Praise for AFTER SCHI

· · · ◆ · · ·

"This is an unflinching account of a family's struggle to care for a schizophrenic adult child, Barb, who languished for 30 years as a homebound invalid. Once her parents died the author and her brother were tenacious and determined to try to find help and improve the state of their now 63-year-old sister's life. It is a heartwarming story of a family's struggle to come to terms with severe mental illness and find hope and love on the other side. What it shows us, once again, is that most of what we think we know about mental illness is just plain wrong."

—MARK VONNEGUT, MD, author of *The Eden Express* and *Just Like Someone Without Mental Illness Only More So*

· · · ◆ · · ·

"I began *After Schizophrenia* wondering if I had the stamina for a book I knew would be fraught with reminders of my own difficult life with my mentally ill sister. But it turned out to be a beautifully crafted story of immense compassion and subtle humor that held me in thrall from the first page to the last. In countless ways, Margaret Hawkins tailored her own life to suit the needs of her family, especially her beloved, charismatic older sister, but one has to read between the lines to grasp the scope of her sacrifices and her devotion. She tells her story with great tenderness, both for her parents who, like most parents, made grave mistakes and for her sister, Barb, who changed from a progressive, funny, sophisticated role model to a shy and shadowy woman haunted by voices she could not control. Because of Margaret's refusal to give up on her, Barb at last reemerges. I loved this generous memoir, a moving testament to optimism and determination."

—MARGARET MOORMAN, author of *My Sister's Keeper*

· · · ◆ · · ·

"In this book, Margaret Hawkins wrenchingly depicts a family crippled by dysfunction and the stigma of mental illness. The loss of Barb to years of psychosis is so sad, but her recovery is inspiring and instructional. What we see so vividly through these pages is that mental illness is treatable, the biggest obstacle being fear and ignorance."

—RICHARD K. BAER, MD, author of *Switching Time*

· · · ◆ · · ·

"*After Schizophrenia* is an honest and engaging portrayal of the often sudden, always life-changing, onset of mental illness—both for the person who experiences it and the family and friends who love her. Lives that seem so promising and so hopeful can be forever changed by mental illness, but *After Schizophrenia* shows us that the change isn't necessarily forever and that there is so much reason to hope. Readers are brought into this family's world through the eyes of a sibling, a perspective that is seldom written about but immensely important, and are shown how life can be turned upside-down and then brought right back to being right-side up by mental illness, empowerment, and the human spirit."

—ALISON K. MALMON, Founder and Executive Director, Active Minds, Inc.

· · · ◆ · · ·

"A moving yet down-to-earth portrayal of what's it like to live with a serious mental illness. Hawkins affirms the hope of recovery for millions of others like Barb."

—LINDA ROSENBERG, MSW, President and CEO, National Council for Community Behavioral Healthcare

· · · ◆ · · ·

"A beautiful tribute to an older sister who hears voices, from the elegant pen of a younger one who never gave up. The steady care on display here is what real love is all about. Their rare story should inspire America's 3 million affected families to keep the faith for the least of our brethren."

—PATRICK TRACEY, author of *Stalking Irish Madness: Searching for the Roots of My Family's Schizophrenia*

After Schizophrenia

After Schizophrenia

The Story of My Sister's Reawakening After 30 Years

Margaret Hawkins

Conari Press

This edition first published in 2011 by Conari Press, an imprint of Red Wheel/
Weiser, LLC
With offices at:
665 Third Street, Suite 400
San Francisco, CA 94107
www.redwheelweiser.com

ISBN: 978-1-57324-535-7
Library of Congress Cataloging-in-Publication Data available upon request

Cover design by Jim Warner

Printed in the United States of America
M
10 9 8 7 6 5 4 3 2 1

The paper used in this publication meets the minimum requirements of the
American National Standard for Information Sciences—Permanence of Paper for
Printed Library Materials Z39.48-1992 (R1997).

For my sister, Barbara

···◆···

And in loving memory of my parents,
Barbara Faxon Hawkins and Thomas Rhodes Hawkins

What we do not make conscious emerges later as fate.

— CARL JUNG

Foreword

When the galley proofs for this book first arrived, with a request to write a foreword, I had just been "fired" as my own twin sister's guardian, conservator, and hospital contact person.

People often think I became a psychiatrist to try to help my sister, but the truth is I became a psychiatrist in spite of her. Unlike Barb Hawkins, whom you're about to meet, Pamela has spent decades in and out of hospitals because of schizophrenia. For many years there was no predicting when an emergency call about her would jolt me out of bed. Never as her doctor, you understand, just as next of kin. Recently she's been in-patient for weeks. Last night, I refused to sign her out AMA (Against Medical Advice), and now I'm persona non grata? I don't know whether to be angry or ecstatic.

As it turns out however, the timing is perfect. Without a hospital visit to Pammy looming, I have hours to spend reading this manuscript with the intriguing title, *After Schizophrenia,* comfortably ensconced on the sofa.

The pages slip quickly by as I welcome Margaret and Barbara and the whole of the Hawkins clan into my home and I almost finish the memoir in one sitting. I've never met Margaret, and yet I feel I know her... *like a sister* is what I say the first time we talk a few days later. Nevertheless, as I read, the puzzling words *home invasion* keep popping into my head. The words usually refer to something *violent,* like breaking and entering. Then I realize--of course, the Hawkins home *and* family *have* been invaded by schizophrenia, just as it invaded my own home years ago, as it has invaded homes for millennia, silently unraveling lives and destroying dreams.

Worse, the stigma of schizophrenia marks entire families as modern-day lepers, alienating many patients *and* caretakers from friends, family and community. Readers of my own book (and Pammy's) *Divided Minds* may remember what stigma did in the early years to the Spiro family. In Ms. Hawkins's book the stigma of schizophrenia is so powerful that Barbara's father has to die before she can get help. To understand what both the Hawkinses and my family experienced years ago, you have to keep in mind that forty years ago many people, even psychiatrists, didn't think of schizophrenia as a bona fide physical brain illness.

When Pammy first got sick in the mid 60's, we were in junior high. Our younger brother and sister were both still in elementary school and our parents had their hands full. Schizophrenia may have been at work in the background *but there was nothing obvious.* Despite hearing voices inside her head, Pammy didn't tell anyone what was happening. Just like Barb Hawkins, for a long time she seemed only depressed or withdrawn, but she didn't act or talk "crazy" in the way most people expect. Gradually though, as she got worse, schizophrenia affected the lives of everyone in the family.

In my second reading of *After Schizophrenia* I focus more on Mr. Hawkins. What kind of man fears doctors so much that he risks his children's well-being and sometimes even their lives? At nine, Margaret herself almost loses a toe because her father refuses to take her to a doctor. Years later, Barb has returned home ill and unable to function; Mr. Hawkins mistrusts psychiatrists at least as much as she does. It is Mr. Hawkins' love-as-best-medicine-twenty-four-hours-a-day, seven days a week, personalized attention to his daughter's care that allows her to go for years without getting professional help. Other parents insist that their adult children undergo treatment *as a condition* of their living at home. He takes pains to do the opposite and it seems to work...

More surprising, a psychiatrist, psychologist, social worker and even probate court judge, despite serious reservations, all go along with him. Why do all these professionals enable him (to borrow a phrase)? Is this stigma? Is this family served or are they neglected by the system? Couldn't *someone* have helped the Hawkins family a long time before? How many illnesses get reduced to whispers in courtrooms like those in which Mr. Hawkins plies his case? If that isn't stigma, what is?

I don't know the answers except that we cannot allow stigma to silence us. That's why books like *After Schizophrenia* are so important. The Hawkins family is just beginning to talk. I hope this book makes it easier for all of us to keep the conversation going.

The devastation schizophrenia wrought in my sister's life and how it changed the direction of mine is the focus of our book, *Divided*

Minds: Twin Sisters and Their Journey Through Schizophrenia, published in the fall of 2005 by St. Martin's Press. Shortly after our memoir came out, we were invited to talk on a National Public Radio show. We arrived at an NYC radio station and were ushered into the waiting area with a few minutes to spare. I sat down next to an elderly gentleman while Pam shuffled to a seat at the far end of the bench. She slumped there, eyes staring at the carpet while her right hand traced figure eights rapidly over and over again into her jeans.

"May I take a look at your book?"

The face was familiar, but the voice was unmistakable. *Art Buchwald.*

I shot him a quick glance, and handed him my copy. He flipped it over and scanned the back cover. Then he thumbed through the book and peppered me with questions about schizophrenia, before lapsing into silence.

A minute before our call came to go on the air he spoke.

"You know," he said, his gravelly voice wavering from age or possibly from emotion, "My mother had schizophrenia. They put her away in an institution for thirty-five years and I never knew her..."

Schizophrenia silenced his mother for sure. But who silenced him and who silences us?

Schizophrenia doesn't silence us. Stigma does, but it shouldn't.

Art Buchwald is gone now, but how many other celebrities will talk publicly about their battles or their relatives' battles with depression, alcoholism, drug abuse, even bipolar disorder, but still won't mention the word schizophrenia? Is schizophrenia the disease "that dare not speak its name?"

In the Spiro family much has changed since 2005. Pammy is welcome at all family gatherings though sometimes *she* chooses not to attend. I hope that our parents now understand that schizophrenia is an illness, a brain disease, *and that it has never been their fault.* I'm sorry that Mr. and Mrs. Hawkins will never get that chance.

When Margaret and I talked, for me it was like talking to a sister I'd never met. We both note that our experiences with sisters with schizophrenia were strikingly similar, as were many experiences in our families even though Barbara is almost a generation older than we are and Pam is my identical twin. I look forward to meeting in person someday soon.

I have come to see schizophrenia as a journey, caregiver or patient, ill or well, family or friend, our journeys differ only in the details.

The more you speak out about the schizophrenia, the easier it becomes.

The more you ask others for help, the less alone you feel.

The more hope you give, the more hope you have.

If stigma were no more, patients like Barb would get earlier treatment and families would not spend years divided. Sisters and brothers, mothers and fathers would not feel like outcasts in their homes and communities.

Untreated schizophrenia has the power to destroy neural connections in the brain, and often much cognitive and interpersonal functioning, but—

Schizophrenia's power to destroy a person, a relationship, a family, is only as great as we allow it to be.

This journey is one I didn't choose, but one I *do* choose to continue. If you're reading this book, I wager, so do you. The truth is, none of us can make this journey of schizophrenia or any journey of life alone. For all the help I've received along the way, I'm grateful more than words can say.

Recently I came across this quote from Albert Schweitzer, "Sometimes our light goes out, but it is blown again into flame by an encounter with another human being. Each of us owes a debt of gratitude to those who have rekindled the light."

Margaret Hawkins's book *After Schizophrenia* has been a light for me. Thank you, Margaret.

My advice: Read this book. If your light isn't blown into flame after reading it the first time, Read It Again. Then, buy it for a friend. As a thank you gift.

BTW, a couple of days ago Pammy called. She's better. She apologized for her anger. Of course, she reinstated me....

—Carolyn S. Spiro, MD, 2010

Acknowledgments

This story and this book wouldn't have been possible without the contributions of many people. Thank you to my agent, Jodie Rhodes, and to Caroline Pincus at Conari Press for believing in this book and to all the people at Conari for making it happen. Thanks to everyone in my sister's life who made her current life possible. Thank you first to Wendy Trafny, who showed up at our darkest hour and finessed the arrangement that remains in place today, and thanks to her organization, New Foundation Center (formerly Wilpower). Thank you to Dr. Weinstein, the kind psychiatrist who came to the house, and to his successor, Dr. Hristea. Thanks to Maria Moreno and Dr. Davis for their kind services. Huge thanks to Yvonne Flowers, who has done so much to help Barb be independent. Thanks to Joyce Garb and everyone at the North Shore Senior Center and to Laura Solomon and Rosa Denton and all the other good people at CMSS—Carol, both Karens, Leticia, Lisa, Chantal. Thanks to everyone at Rainbow Hospice. Thanks to Norwood Drugs, the Illinois Food Bank, and Meals on Wheels. Thanks to Deb Ekstrom, John Spear, and Amy Smith for professional advice. Thanks to all my father's friends, neighbors, and fellow church members for including Barb in their lives and thoughts—Amy Crawford, Paul and Pat Adlaf, Richard and Susan Coad, Pat and Bob Tambourino, to name only some. Thanks to Diane, Cari, Kim, Marty, Sandy, and Steph for visiting. Thanks to Sylvia for sending many home-baked cookies and much good cheer. Thanks to all my friends who've been so encouraging in this long endeavor—your support has meant so much. Thanks to Louise Young, who read this when it felt most impossible. Thanks to Barb's friends, Sandy and Dieter Britz, and to Henry Bauer for helping me research Karim. Thanks to Maria and Milind Kulkarni for lending me their house (and their dog, Maxie) during the crucial editing stage. Thank you to Fritz for all the food, favors, and cheer he's brought to Barb, not to mention the changed light bulbs, hammered pots, sawed firewood, fixed doorbells, and general technical support.

Thank you finally to Tom for going along with my impossible dream for Barb.

PART I
1943 – 2006

Chapter One

On a promising summer day in 1974, my family's life blew up, though we didn't know it at the time. That was the day my beautiful, bright, and very American older sister returned home from Iraq.

We hadn't seen Barb in nearly three years, not since she and her Iraqi husband had moved to Basra in the summer of 1971. She'd been a radiant twenty-seven-year-old seemingly in her prime when Karim, finished with his two-year post-doctoral appointment at the University of Kentucky and unable to find a job in the States, was offered a full professorship in chemistry at Basra University. He'd had qualms about returning to the Middle East, but he wanted the job, so my sister, in love and eager for adventure, gamely went along.

Now three years later our beautiful Barb, the family star, was back for a visit. Except, she wasn't. Something had changed during those years she was gone, and the Barb we knew never really returned. The woman my parents collected at the airport that June day, whom I rushed home from college on a Greyhound bus to welcome back, was not the Barb any of us remembered saying goodbye to three years before. That Barb had vanished, and though her husband tried to bring her home, she was already gone, schizophrenic.

For the next thirty-two years, Barb lived, some might say languished, in the house she came home to—first with my parents and then, after my mother died, alone with my father until his death at the age of eighty-nine in December 2006. During that time she was never hospitalized, never evaluated by a psychiatrist, never prescribed medication, and after the first few years, she never left the house. Then suddenly my father was gone, I was her guardian, and both our lives were changing fast. I had no idea what would happen next, no idea that the dark tunnel we'd entered in June of 1974 was about to open into light.

But to explain how extraordinary these changes were—and continue to be—I need to go back to the beginning of the story, to the beginning of my sister's journey from suburban Chicago to Basra, Iraq, through schizophrenia, and back.

···◆···

My sister was born in 1943 and grew up as the eldest of three children in a conservative, comfortable commuter suburb north of Chicago known in those days for its good schools and quiet streets. Three years later my brother, Tom, was born, and then eight years after that, when my sister was eleven, I arrived. We were a family of five, six if you count George the dog.

My real memories of Barb don't begin until I was four or five, when she was almost out of high school. Memory isn't always—or even often—real, though, and many of my recollections are composites constructed from family stories collaged together with pictures taken before I was born or at least before my own memories began to form.

I studied these photos as a child, memorized them as I sat on the floor leafing back and forth through the wide, black pages of big photo albums, trying to piece together what happened before I was there to see for myself. I'd come late to the party, and I could never learn enough about Barb, who always seemed to slip out the door just as I was arriving and who left for college when I was starting second grade. I could never catch up with her, and even before anything overtly strange happened, she was mysterious to me in ways that made me try to understand her without simply asking, which didn't seem possible. Instead, I chose the more indirect and secretive process of spying on the past through the peephole of someone else's camera lens.

Photographs of my sister as a child show a dreamy, pretty, dark-haired girl with a willowy figure and a faraway gaze in her big gray stunned-looking eyes. Even when she is smiling in the photos, which she often isn't, she appears distracted by some thought or only half awake, affable but abstractly so.

One early photo shows Barb with my father at a Camp Fire Girls father-daughter dinner. Maybe she is eight or nine. She wears her uniform, complete with a vest full of earnestly stitched-on patches and leans wispily, almost shyly, toward my father who, in his business suit at the end of a long day in the financial district, looks gruff and a little combative. Another photo, taken about the same time, shows my sister and brother looking waifish and sweet with their heads tilted together, tucked into a narrow bed with all their dolls and toys. There are studio portraits with Santa and a Halloween snapshot showing seven-year-old Tom, in my father's fedora, sticking my sister in the ribs with a toy gun. Ten-year-old Barb, always a bit dramatic, leans back to expose her vulnerable neck in a fair pantomime of death.

In the early photos, my mother, a cool, smoky beauty, looks lushly voluptuous in her shirtwaist dresses and pearls as she presides over cascades of children. She shows up less often and less happily later on. Off to the side stands my father, always in a suit, suspenders, and a crooked bowtie; he frowns and bites down on the stem of his pipe.

The surroundings in these photos are telling. Here we are, the so-called prosperous middle class, but of a sort constrained by WASP reserve and thrift. Our furniture is solid and old, slightly beat up and mostly passed down, with no sign of the 1950s anywhere except in my mother's waist-cinching dresses and my brother's ubiquitous Danny O'Day ventriloquist puppet. In the background, details of our genteel but already crumbling old house are visible—wide molding, bay windows, brick fireplace. What doesn't show is what isn't there and won't ever be. Modern conveniences—dishwasher, garbage disposal, laundry dryer, garage door opener, air conditioner—were not for us.

The pace of regular family photo taking quickened when Barb received a camera around the age of eleven. Even though she's not in many of the photos from that era, the subjects she chose reveal the texture of what appears to have been her very normal life. Two album pages devoted to My Slumber Party show a dozen or so grinning girls in pajamas and braces, circa 1955, lying in various arranged patterns on the floor. There are photos of George, looking like a canine tornado barely contained on a kitchen chair, and there's a whole page titled Baby Margaret, in which I appear as a somber, glowing bundle propped against various chair backs wearing a too-large cowboy hat.

Fortunately Tom got seriously interested in cameras early on so there are pictures of Barb too. One shows her standing on a beach in a wet, baggy bathing suit, straight and skinny as a stick. Another shows her at twelve or thirteen sitting on our scratchy old couch in a tight-bodiced, full-skirted party dress that shows off her slim figure. She wears a bow at her neck and appears perfectly symmetrical except for the slight, ingratiating tilt of her head that softens the pose from stiff to winsome. In another she stands on a tennis court, rail thin in shorts with a racket dangling from one wiry arm. Another shows her sitting at the secondhand Story & Clark upright piano my father bought her when she started taking lessons. She's a little older here, maybe fourteen, and fresh faced with her wrists raised gracefully over the keys. She smiles at the photographer over her shoulder. Behind her, we see sheet music for show tunes.

What strikes me most about these photos now is how cooperative my sister looks, how sweet. Childhood pictures of me show a different sort of child, a small girl with her hand on her hip and her eyebrows knitted, with one corner of her mouth raised in a wary half smile. I look challenging, intense, wry, dubious, cautious, worried. But Barb appears soft and unfailingly compliant, not eager to please, exactly, but willing to if asked. I look for clues in these photos but, honestly, other than a bit of dreaminess, I don't find them. All they're proof—and reminder—of is that her life, her many activities, her friends, and even we, her family, were once apparently quite normal.

Then the Barb in these photos changes. She goes from being a dreamy sylph, often photographed with my brother, who even as a small boy looks perpetually droll, to a stunning and self-aware young woman. Here is where the photos and my actual memories of Barb converge. She's fifteen, sixteen, seventeen, and though her figure never seems to really fill out—she'll be thin her whole life—she blooms, and her face sharpens a little. There is a new confidence, a consciousness of her own beauty.

Here is a photo I often returned to as a child, taken at some family gathering. It shows Barb sitting in the midst of a whirl of activity, detached and unsmiling. She wears dark lipstick and her dark hair is held back in a high severe ponytail tied with a crisp ribbon. She holds a Pepsi bottle and turns away from the camera, her elegant neck swiveling to show us her haughty profile, her slender legs crossed in a tight skirt. Here is the actual Barb I remember, suddenly a high school goddess.

In the background I see a blur of swinging white blond hair, me. I look about five, which means it would have been the year my mother's mother walked into the lake to die. Barb would have been sixteen. It is impossible to find the impact of that event in any of these photos except for the fact of my mother's absence from them for a long time.

Then a yellowed newspaper clipping dated a year later picks up the thread. It's a rave review of *Publicity Mad*, the story of aspiring actresses in Greenwich Village—that year's senior class play. Tucked in the back of the photo album along with the review is the program, which indicates that Barb Hawkins played a beatnik named Marcille Benedict.

My earliest memory of my sister in real time is Christmas morning when I was five and she was sixteen. She gave me an enormous stuffed bear I named Timmy, a grand gesture. The summer before, she'd had her first job; she must have felt flush, generous. Every year after that she gave me a different oversized stuffed animal, next a dog named Sam, and then a lion I named Gunther.

In these early memories my sister is nearly a young woman, and to me a distant figure, as radiant and unapproachable as a god, and as dangerous and capricious as one too, to be adored and feared. She was even less interested in homemaking than my mother was, and this indifference—she let it be known—included children. I don't think she ever babysat, and she wouldn't cook. The only concession she made to the domestic arts was to sew, and though she became very good at it, covering the dining room table with expanses of starchy-smelling stiff fabric pinned with tissue paper patterns I was not allowed touch, it was for her love of clothes and design, not out of any interest in housewifery.

I remember her clothes in aggregate but also as individual garments. I remember circle skirts and straight plaid ones hanging in her closet, and her neat piles of thick, bleached-white bobby socks. She kept a box of rolled silk hair ribbons on her dresser organized by color and ironed to perfection, and she wore them to match her outfits, tied in bows around the rubber bands that kept her ponytail in place. When she wasn't there I stole into her room to fondle them though she would have been furious if she'd known.

I remember her stacks of sweaters, first short-waisted ones with three-quarter-length sleeves and tiny pearlescent buttons down the front and later bulky mohair sweaters in every pastel color piled up in drawers that reeked of mothballs. Pink, cream, turquoise, chocolate, lavender, big and puffy on her tiny frame, all the rage in the 1960s. I remember her sewing machine and the clothes she made on it, the beautiful things she couldn't afford to buy, and I remember the beautiful things she did buy when she started working.

One summer she worked as a supervisor at the park district and came home tan and sinewy every day at noon in a white blouse and navy shorts that showed off her pretty legs. She'd sit at the kitchen table and wolf down mountains of food—ham salad, macaroni salad, and something called Hawaiian salad made from marshmallows, coconut, and mayonnaise that my mother bought at Barb's imperious request and, after that, big slabs of Sara Lee cheesecake—her dark brown ponytail swinging arrogantly as she complained about the brats she had to supervise. I was afraid of her that summer, afraid I was too much one of the brats she hated. Being near her was like getting too close to a fire. I might be burned by her random wrath or just by the heat from her immortal glow. She did glow, the red lipstick, the shiny hair, the perfect white teeth—she was as formidable and thoughtlessly cruel as any perfect sixteen-year-old girl could be.

In the summers she lay in a plastic lawn chair in the back yard wearing big dark glasses and reading fashion magazines, wetting her finger on her tongue before turning each page with a dramatic flick, hoping for boys to walk by so she could snub them. I remember how the house smelled of her perfume every morning and how the smell of it as she got ready for high school blended chokingly with the salty smell of bacon as my mother sadly cooked breakfast. Barb played tennis well enough to win trophies, played bridge with her friends, and played boogie-woogie on the piano.

More than four decades later, I dig her high school senior yearbook, dated 1961, out of a pile in the pantry. When I open it a cloud of mildew escapes, but there, untouched by time, is my sister's shining face on every other page. Here, she is kneeling in the front row of a group shot of girl gym leaders, smiling adorably. There, she is editing the school newspaper. On another page, she poses with the aspiring writers on the *Wet Paint* staff and on the next with members of the Quill and Scroll Society. Here she is yet again, twice, in a double-page spread on the school play, dressed all in black, reclining on a couch at center stage, staring moodily at the camera as the rest of the act unfolds around her.

Her face leaps out clear and bright among all these faces, most of which, in that era of helmet hairdos and terrible clothes, look strange and lost. My sister, though, looks neither strange nor lost. She looks anointed by luck, not only beautiful but self-aware, put together, confident, and even well coifed. Most of these others will grow up and out of their awkwardness into their own beauty and beautiful lives, but my sister's life is reversed, it begins with beauty. She appears not to have had an awkward day in her life.

Next to my sister's senior picture is a list of her school activities, the longest on the page. *Barbara Hawkins: Pioneer [year] 4, Feature Editor 4; Senior Class Play 4; Gym Leader 3, 4; Quill and Scroll 4; Creative Writing Magazine 4; Class Council Representative 1; '61 Blueprint Staff 3; Biology Club 1, Social Chairman 1; Future Teachers Club 3; G.A.A. 1, 2; Chemistry Club 2; French Club 3; Stagecrafters Club 1.*

Underneath this formidable catalog of accomplishments and memberships—social chairman for the biology club!—Barb has added her own list in blue ink. It names her activities outside of school: Model on Fashion Board, Church Choir, Corresponding Secretary for Community Church Youth Group. My heart seizes at the sight of this careful addition which, written so purposefully in her neat, round, girlish hand, reminds me of her patch-filled Camp Fire

Girls vest. Both are proof of how much she cared about belonging, doing, and achieving.

Then she was off to college at the University of Illinois. What I remember about that year is not her absence but the way the house, and particularly my father, filled with excitement when she came home. On the Friday evenings of her arrivals television was banned. Instead of watching *Route 66,* as I would have preferred, we sat in a circle and watched Barb tell stories as if she were Marco Polo. Everything in her telling was larger than life—her professors, her friends, the books she was reading. Everybody and everything was *brilliant,* the world was wide, and she loved her life away from us.

Midway through her sophomore year, Barb came home and stayed for three semesters. She'd been put on academic probation. The official story was some combination of too much fun, too many boyfriends, too much homework. Now it seems like it may have been something darker but it's impossible to know whether her coming home was a retreat or a reining in. Maybe, probably, my father had insisted.

She lived in her old room that year and commuted to the city branch of the university by train. It must have been difficult to come home after the freedom and exhilaration of being away, and I remember her in those days sitting on her bed smoking an endless succession of cigarettes, which she sometimes shared with me, although I was only nine. My father displayed a new frustration with her that year, complaining that she dragged her feet when they walked to the train together in the morning. He preferred military bearing and a crisp marching gait.

These days, I search for the thing—the sign that tells me the sickness had begun. Was this it, this early, I wonder now, brought on by the stresses of being away at college, or was it just a normal phase in her young life? Was my father being overbearing and intrusive, trying to curtail her independence, or helpful in insisting she come home?

Or did she want to come home? Looking back, it seems strange that this bright, socially successful, ambitious girl would suddenly move back into her childhood bedroom just as her life outside it had begun.

Whatever the reason, though, I liked having her there, particularly when she signed up for biology and brought home her own rat to dissect on the kitchen table. We named him Boris and kept him in the pantry. The kitchen smelled of formaldehyde that winter.

One day, without preamble, she sat me down on her bed, drew a uterus and some fallopian tubes in her spiral notebook, and explained the female reproductive system to me. It must have been on her mind, possibly the result of the same biology class that required her to carve up poor Boris, but maybe she had more practical reasons as well. As for me, at nine, my interest was purely theoretical, though I was glad to be the first among my friends to know.

This was 1963. She wore perfume and lipstick, no other makeup or jewelry, with black turtleneck sweaters and wheat-colored jeans. She started to wear her long hair loose and wild, no more neat ponytails. She listened to Barbra Streisand, turned up loud on the rickety portable record player in her bedroom. She talked about Bob Dylan. She dated a succession of fascinating—to me—men including an Arab named Maurice who came to pick her up at the house once dressed in a dark suit. I was so intrigued I named one of my trolls after him. She dated lots of men but, as she had in high school, seemed scornful of them, accepting their gifts but dodging their calls and disparaging their attentions. Men were louts and a little beneath her, her behavior seemed to suggest. She made it clear she didn't plan to get snared by a life of love, marriage, and motherhood.

Chapter Two

In the fall of her senior year, Barb went back downstate to finish her degree, and that's when she met Karim Shallal, a shy graduate student working on his master's of science degree in analytical chemistry. On their first date he took her to an ice show and when the clowns released a bunch of balloons from a polka-dotted box mounted on skates, he caught the purple one and gave it to her. That balloon did it, she said, and it was to be the first of many, many gifts. He brought oranges to her dorm room, which she kept on the windowsill next to her portable Shakespeare. He cooked for her. He taught her how to make rice so it wouldn't get soggy. And when she went to his apartment and saw the wooden camels he'd positioned in a caravan across the top of his refrigerator, she cried. She could see he was homesick. Later she wrote a poem about it, about a lonely girl forced to choose between love and independence. It was 1965. It never occurred to her she could have both.

We met Karim when Barb graduated from college, with a degree in English and a minor in history. My parents and brother and I drove to Champaign to attend the commencement ceremony, and afterward we went to a picnic given by Karim and his fellow graduate students in the chemistry department who were celebrating their own graduation.

There are pictures of us at this picnic, and unlike the earlier ones in the family album, these are in color. There I am, ten years old in crooked bangs and a sleeveless blue A-line dress, but mostly they are of Barb, radiant Barb, first in her cap and gown and later sitting in the grass at the picnic accepting a Technicolor slice of bright pink watermelon from Karim. She's wearing plaid Bermuda shorts, a sleeveless orange knit sweater, matching orange lipstick, and her first short haircut, which my parents lamented and which suited her so well. Karim, in his standard white shirt, baggy black pants, and thick black-rimmed glasses, looks shy and professorial as he hands her the slice. The color in these photos matters—she is creamy white and he is nut brown.

Here is what I remember of our first meeting.

Karim: How do you like Champaign?

Me: I prefer beer.

Karim impressed me, and I was bent on impressing him back, on holding my own. Everyone laughed, and someone had to explain to me why. As the youngest I was used to being teased, but what I remember is that he was kind. I liked him.

I was eleven when they got engaged. Karim came to dinner at our house one night and after dessert he proposed marriage, formally, to my parents. Where he got the idea to do that, I don't know. Maybe Barb told him he had to, or maybe it was natural to him, coming from an even more patriarchal culture than the one my father had tried to institute in our house. I say *tried* because my mother and I—my brother was off the hook—were hard cases, my mother because she retreated into elusiveness and me because I was headstrong and rebellious. Neither of us accorded my father what he deemed his proper respect. Only Barb did that.

Barb was twenty-two when they got engaged. It was a great romance, or so it seemed to me. Karim had courted her for almost two years, first in Champaign then later long distance while he worked on his doctorate in Lexington, Kentucky. Barb had moved home after graduation and taken a job as a secretary at Encyclopedia Britannica, once again commuting into the city with my father every morning. She'd started out with editorial aspirations but, after the engagement, boning up on Karim's culture became her focus. She signed up for Arabic classes and took to reading *The Alexandria Quartet* on the train into the city every morning.

I wonder now what my parents thought of all this. I thought Karim was handsome. He dressed more formally than most American men his age, in pressed white cotton shirts and dark, loose, elegantly tailored trousers. He had graceful posture, smooth carmelly skin, and dark eyes behind thick glasses that gave him an appealing air of abstraction and vulnerability. He combed his black hair straight back on his scalp; he was a little old world.

I tried to interpret him to my friends who wanted all the details when I told them about the engagement. My friend Sandy's older sister Sharon, who was fifteen and whom I admired for owning the biggest collection of Beatles paraphernalia I'd ever seen, asked me if he was cute. I tried to explain, but I had no words for how appealing I found his formal manners, his finely manicured hands, and the courtly, besotted way he behaved around my sister. Yes, I said, as a default answer, but it wasn't quite true. He wasn't cute, I might have said if I could have formed the thought, but he was beautiful.

There was a tender interlude between the engagement and the wedding. Karim brought gifts and sent flowers. I remember regular deliveries of candy and record albums—mostly sweet, sixties-style string arrangements of romantic melodies—all inscribed "To My Sweat Heart." Tom and I howled, but Barb never corrected his spelling.

Karim visited on weekends, taking the train up from Lexington when he could get away from his research. He stayed at a hotel, and they went on dates in the city, returning home with doggie bags and matchbooks bearing the names of famous restaurants. Once they went to a museum and brought back a present for me—three silk butterfly hair clips. It had never occurred to me I could inspire such an exotic, feminine gift. The bounty of my sister's romance was overflowing onto me.

After the engagement, my father announced he'd hired a private detective to investigate Karim. Nothing personal, he said, just due diligence, necessitated by the difference between our cultures. We hadn't met his family, knew nothing of him but what he'd told us. It wasn't unreasonable, and Karim apparently didn't mind or at least didn't object. Time passed, and when nothing untoward was discovered, plans for the wedding proceeded.

Forty years later, as my father lay dying, I told him how conscientious I thought it had been, both to hire the detective and to let it be known that he had. I'd meant to comfort him, but all those years later, weeks away from death, my father refused to be comforted. Nothing I did or said could ever make up for what he'd lost: Barb.

"That moron was useless," he spat from his hospital bed. "He didn't uncover one goddamn thing I didn't already know."

One of my father's favorite jokes in later years: *Just because you're paranoid doesn't mean everybody isn't out to get you.* He must already have sensed danger back in 1966, but he was looking for it in the wrong direction. Karim wasn't the disaster that was about to derail my sister's life.

Though maybe he was a sign of its approach. For a sheltered American girl with feminist leanings to marry a man from so far away, from a culture so different and so deeply misogynistic, now seems like an odd and reckless decision, especially for a girl who seemed to have so many choices. Barb and Karim clearly loved each other, but the whole thing might never have happened if Barb's judgment hadn't already begun to fail.

And she seemed to know it. It's impossible now to separate her dramatic ambivalence from early signs of mental illness, but at the very least, Barb had taken a lot of winning over. She ran hot and cold, made Karim pursue her, shunned him, dumped him, took him back, and disparaged everything about marriage. If Karim had only wanted to marry a pretty American, he could have found someone easier. Almost anyone would have been easier.

Even after the engagement, Barb made it clear she wasn't interested in being a conventional bride. She bought the first wedding dress she tried on—the Halloween Costume, she called it—lost all interest in china shopping after my father vetoed her wildly expensive first choice, and wanted no part in planning the wedding. (Nor did my mother. I believe the dubious honor fell to my father, by default.) She refused to learn how to cook, swore up and down she would never have children, and told me, her easily impressed eleven-year-old confidante, that she planned to take lovers and keep naked men standing at attention around the house to serve her grapes. Karim weathered all this and probably a lot more.

Certainly it was unusual behavior for a bride, especially in the sixties, but we just thought Barb was high-spirited and independent. Looking back, though, it seems like she was fighting a tide stronger than convention, trying to keep her head up for one last gasp of independence before sinking down into the drowning seas of what she saw as her womanly fate. And for her, that fate wasn't just the danger of losing her identity to the role of wife to an older, strong-minded, Middle Eastern man, but the danger of losing it to a creeping, secret condition that would strip much more from her than any husband could. Marriage was scary enough, especially in the shadow of my parents' difficult union, but for her it was the coincidental point of passage into something much darker.

I wonder now if she already knew she was ill, and if that made her equate love with madness, an equation which, after all, is not so farfetched or without precedent. I wonder if her irreverence and resistance were early signs of illness or the opposite, a struggle against it for health and self-knowledge. Or maybe it was just a sign of the times. It seems strange now—why not just break off the engagement if she wasn't sure? But I think she didn't feel she could. She believed love meant surrender and suffering, even without knowing how ill she was or that she was headed for Iraq. Besides, for a good girl in my family in 1966, marriage was the only way out of the house.

Somehow the wedding came together, and on December 31, 1966, Barb married Karim in a small chapel at the same church my sister had attended as a girl. How strange it felt for Karim, a Muslim at least by culture if not by practice, I'll never know. The late-afternoon reception was at home, simple. Nielsen's Restaurant catered it. The menu was champagne, shrimp cocktail, and hot Swedish meatballs in a chafing dish. There were red candles on the mantle and Arab scientists everywhere. I still remember some of their names—Salah and his American wife, Nancy; Karim's best man, George Al-Bazzi; and a boyish young chemist named Raoul.

Barb had one bridesmaid, her college friend Jain, who wore a chic red velvet cocktail-length sheath, a seasonal choice. I was a junior bridesmaid in a smashing dropped-waist dress with cream lace on top and a flared red velvet skirt. Somewhere there is a photo of me at twelve with long hair and short bangs holding up a champagne glass tipsily. Surrounded by dark, dashing men, I look like Alice in Wonderland at an Arabian singles bar.

Later that night Barb changed into a fitted pink mohair suit and she and Karim left for a hotel. A delayed honeymoon to Niagara Falls followed in the spring, pictures from which show them huddled in yellow slickers on a narrow ledge as sheets of water sluice down around them.

Before the wedding, Barb had shipped a few things to Kentucky—she didn't own much—and immediately afterward moved from her childhood bedroom in suburban Chicago into Karim's tiny apartment in Lexington without any interval of independent living. Except for two-and-a-half years away at college and a three-week post-graduation trip to Europe, Barb had never been on her own. Even her campus years had been protected and supervised. She'd lived in an all-girls dorm where regulations outnumbered responsibilities. There were curfews in those days, house rules, structured social activities, group meals.

Newly married at twenty-three, she had never paid rent, never cooked or bought her own groceries, never owned a car, never managed her own money for her own financial support. She'd never had an apartment, the decor and upkeep of which—let alone the comings and goings of overnight guests from which—would have been entirely up to her. She had never lived her life on her own terms without someone else with more power and more money to be accountable to, and now she was moving on to be managed by someone else.

In 1966, Barb's inexperience wasn't uncommon, but what may have been was that she moved directly into someone else's already established home. Barb and Karim were newlyweds, but they didn't start out as equals. Karim was no boy. We never knew his exact age— he always said he didn't know it himself—but he had been on his own for years, and Barb moved into a life that was in many ways already set. As with her earlier hiatus from campus life, it now makes me wonder if it was my sister or the illness that made the choice. Was marriage to Karim a retreat from independence that signified her growing unease in the world? Or was it an ill-considered rush into a different kind of independence—marriage? Or was it just how it had to be in 1966?

Barb and Karim's standard-issue university-subsidized graduate student apartment in Lexington was minimal—stark, even—with three rooms, green cinder block walls, and a galley kitchen, but I don't remember Barb ever complaining. She seemed happy there. Minimalism suited her. She'd always loved nice clothes, but beyond that she wasn't particularly interested in things. Every day, Karim walked to the lab—they didn't buy a car until after he finished his PhD in 1969—while Barb stayed home and tried to write, sending stories and poems to magazines, sometimes receiving acceptance letters. Then she got a clerical job at Prudential Insurance Company and tried to write on weekends.

And there they lived, surrounded by like-minded academics, for four-and-a-half apparently happy years. Barb called us every weekend. I remember once coming home from church on a Sunday morning to pick up the ringing phone and hear her voice. She sounded wistful, as if she missed us. I remember because it surprised me. I couldn't understand why she missed us when her life seemed perfect to me.

They visited sometimes at holidays, and we visited them—my father nervously piloting our baby blue VW Beetle, the first new car we'd ever owned—down through the increasingly verdant landscape until we reached the Kentucky border and began to spot green hills and pie shops out the car windows. They showed us the sights—Natural Bridge State Park, horse farms, the racetrack. Karim cooked for us.

I loved being there, and my sister suggested I come back on my own, so I saved up for a plane ticket to make my first trip the summer I was fourteen. It felt wonderful to travel alone, free of my sparring parents and the pedestrian woes of high school, catered to by my indulgent and, as I saw her, incomparably sophisticated sister. The next summer, I went back.

We fell into a happy routine when I was there. Every night, Karim cooked dinner and Barb made the salad, which they ate together from the same bowl. After dinner most nights we walked to a nearby ice cream shop and then, after Karim went to bed, Barb and I sat up late, talking and smoking.

We must have talked about many things, but what I remember now is how Barb spoke about love. There was an intensity about those conversations that was thrilling, and not only because the topic verged on sex.

If, before she was married, she'd been derisive of men and dismissive of the prospect of being a wife, afterward her romanticism bordered on the mystical. She used the word *erotic* a lot. And she was intensely interested in my romances too. When I told her about the progress of a flirtation with a boy I liked, she nodded knowingly and summed it up as "raw passion," simultaneously upgrading a high school crush and sounding like a dentist diagnosing a dead tooth. When I told her my middle-aged teacher had sent me a poem he'd written, something I dimly sensed was a little odd, she made the startling observation that if things kept up, perhaps I would find myself caring for him in his old age. I never knew if she was cagily advising me to discourage his attentions or if she simply saw romantic prospects everywhere, even in the oddest places. Particularly in the oddest places.

On the days my sister worked, I walked around campus and explored used bookstores, once picking up a tattered copy of *Gone with the Wind*, the overheated tone of which matched our nighttime conversations. On other days, when it was too hot to go outside, I stayed home in their air conditioned apartment—a luxury since air conditioning was verboten in our house—reading paperback novels, writing letters, or listening to my sister's records while I baked cakes in their little kitchen. Barb was as delighted as a child to find them when she came home. As ever, she didn't care much for cooking, but she loved to eat.

They treated me like an adult. They took me to a dinner theater, and the three of us shared a bottle of Cold Duck—Barb and I drank most of it. They took me to the movies, and while we watched Goldie Hawn cavort with Walter Matthau, I secretly admired Barb's profile in the dark as she laughed out loud. If her heightened emotion was out of sync with the conventional plot, foreshadowing darker things, I didn't notice. She was my charismatic older sister and I was having the time of my life.

By the next summer, though, everything had changed. Karim's research appointment was up, and when he was offered a teaching post at Basra University, to begin in the fall, they decided to go. Barb was staying with us as a kind of long goodbye.

However upsetting this was to my parents, I think we all assumed the move was temporary. They'd be back, Barb of course, but Karim also. He was part of our family by then. We could no more imagine him disappearing into the Middle East than we could imagine my sister doing so.

They closed up their place in Lexington by August, and while Karim came and went, monitoring his work and staying with friends, Barb hung around the house, lapsing into a languid, passive version of herself I'd never seen. Except for a trip to Just Jeans to buy matching bellbottoms, I don't remember those last days being much fun. A cloud hung over us all.

We didn't discuss it, though, any more than we discussed anything else that troubled us that summer. It was 1971; my brother had been in the Navy for three years, during the worst of the Vietnam War. I was sixteen and going my own kind of crazy, stuck home alone with my parents. My mother was battling the twin demons of her depression—exhaustion and paralyzing indecision—and my father was drinking. Barb's departure for the Middle East was just one more worry in a catalog of them.

Then one day we all went off to the airport and came back without Barb and Karim. If there were tears, I don't remember them. That's how my parents handled pain, with a stiff upper lip, a stiff drink, and a big fight about something else. And besides, Barb seemed happy, off on another adventure.

Chapter Three

My sister was a writer, and as soon as she arrived in Iraq she began writing letters home. At first we received a letter a week, sometimes more, and though the pace slowed a little after the first few months, we continued to receive letters the entire time she was there.

What changed was their tone. At first they were excited, almost delirious, loaded with sensuous detail and breathless description—the languor, the heat, the smell of stewing lamb, the sound of the mullah calling the faithful to prayer. I got a postcard once that simply said "Basra is a pulsating city!" And Barb didn't just luxuriate in the pleasures of their newly comfortable life—which now included servants—she railed at the inequities, the poverty, the educational deprivation, the treatment of women. Her letters were packed with gossip about friends, family, neighbors, colleagues, servants, a cast of characters we could hardly imagine and yet whom she seemed to have fallen in love with instantly. She was full of schemes to make money, literary ambitions, fulminations about everything from the harshness of the Iraqi class structure to women's lib, literary references, rhapsodies about food, requests for American merchandise with brands and sizes included, newspaper clippings, poems, ideas for poems, encouragements, and queries about our lives, and always, always her familiar high-pitched enthusiasm.

She wrote repeatedly about the internal conflict of Western-educated men who'd returned to Iraq to teach at the university and wanted to help their countrymen but hated their country's backward ways, a conflict she knew ate at Karim. She worried about the plight and place of Iraqi women. She told us about her growing closeness with Karim's elderly father, described how he'd presided over the slaughter of a lamb in honor of their new Peugeot, then blessed the car with its blood and gave the meat away. She told how they hired someone to teach them to drive it—it was a stick shift—and boasted that she was learning faster than Karim.

She wrote about their travels through Syria, Lebanon, and Kuwait, described seeing a late model Chevrolet parked in the middle of the desert next to a Bedouin tent. She wrote about her visits to tailors to buy fabric and have dresses made, which she designed. She told us about her jobs—she was determined to work—first in the registrar's office at the university and then in the library, and finally, briefly, in the English department. What her letters didn't mention was why or when that job suddenly ended, offering only a cryptic and belated answer to a question from one of us.

After about a year Barb's letters started to change, coinciding with her sudden and unexplained departure from her last job. Once so vivid and concrete, my sister's writing now sounded veiled, abstract, mystical. She started to talk about telepathy, referring repeatedly to her psychic powers. Now I know that a sudden interest in the supernatural can signal the onset of mental illness, but in those days, in the psychedelic early 1970s, it seemed timely. And besides, my mother and I had always tended to the mystical. Why not Barb now too?

She seemed to lapse into a kind of mesmerized tedium, her letters filled with monotonous descriptions of passive entertainments, endless shopping trips and vacations, repeated visits to tailors to buy ever more clothes, colorless outings to casinos and clubs. She described the weather and the food in these later letters, but the people—that cast of characters she had so vividly detailed before—suddenly and simply disappeared. Then at the end of May 1974, she wrote one last letter, and it was simply hollow.

May 31, 1974

Dear Mom and Dad,

How are you. Last night we went to a party. It was OK. Amel is here today. She's doing some sewing at our house. Some day I'll have to get back to sewing.

It's a very cloudy day. Perhaps it will rain.

We attended graduation exercises. Thank God it wasn't too long and arduous. They held it outside so it wasn't suffocating. Another year is over and no one has anything to say about summer. I don't have much to say now. More later.

Love, Barb.

When my father died, almost thirty-three years after Barb wrote that last letter, I cleared his clothes out of the small, neat upstairs bedroom he'd moved to in his later years, and there, in his dresser, I found a cache of dozens of these letters sequestered in the back of his sock drawer. Written on onionskin paper or lightweight blue air letters and covered with colorful Iraqi postage stamps, they looked to me like treasure buried behind rows of neatly folded brown socks, treasure that might contain the secret of my sister's life. With the racing heart and trembling hands of a detective who has finally found the last, case-solving clue, I scooped them into a deep shopping bag and rushed home to read.

But if I'd expected revelation and epiphany, all I got was frustration. Instead of revealing my sister's secret, the letters simply confirmed her disappearance. Reading them, in order, some thirty years after they were written was like reading a mystery in which suspense builds but the crime is never solved, the culprit never caught. Who stole Barbara's soul? None of the usual suspects.

Chapter Four

One June weekend when I was nineteen, I took a Greyhound bus home from college to attend my sister's homecoming. The academic year was over, and she and Karim had returned for a summer-long visit after nearly three years in Iraq.

I was in summer school and I must have had classes or had to work at my waitressing job at the Chuck Wagon Diner because by the time I got to the house they'd already been home for a few days. Things were not going well. My mother took me aside and told me in a worried whisper that something was wrong. When she and my father had met them at the airport, she said, Barb hadn't known them. She'd called out my name, mistaking other people for me. Maybe, I think now, she was time traveling, seeing her own future. Maybe she already knew what I suspected but what took me thirty-three years to accept, that she and I were to be linked in some special way. Years later I tell this story to my friend Deb, and she says maybe Barb was just thinking, *Who the hell is going to get me out of this mess?* We laugh, nervously, but it's pretty much the same thing.

That weekend is a blur, but I remember a few things. I remember my stunned, wild-eyed, starved-looking sister sitting in a lawn chair in the back yard in the sweltering Chicago summer heat—the same lawn chair she'd occupied so regally in her high school goddess days—eating fancy ice cream out of a big bowl. My already thrifty father—saving for her future would later become his obsession—went wild that weekend buying all her favorite foods, anything he imagined she might want to eat, and waiting on her like a desperate suitor.

I remember my mother hovering, worrying, withdrawing. I recall my brother, who'd flown in from North Carolina for the weekend. He must have been poor, after four years in the Navy and just out of an MFA writing program, but he made the trip. I remember trying to explain to my boyfriend Mike why I couldn't see him that weekend even though he was working in Chicago that summer and I'd be in town for two days. I tried to explain, tearfully, over the phone, the monumental strangeness of what was happening, but there were no words for it.

What I do not remember is Karim. Later he and I would become confidantes whose common interest was Barb and whose common enemy was my father, but that first weekend he faded into the background, nervous, exhausted, self-medicated, and under suspicion, the bearer of very bad news. What was he doing, feeling, saying? We'll never know. Karim has disappeared and, though I've tried to track him down, none of us has heard from him since 1977.

The center of all this family commotion, of course, was my sister, and yet it was she who was not quite there. The charismatic and beautiful, charming and witty Barb, the one who could attract and hold the attention of any group any time, was nowhere to be seen, and in her place was this strange, tiny, cowering person, the ghost of the girl we remembered. It wasn't only that she looked different— haunted and confused, pale and a little hunched over, gaunt instead of just thin with her smooth jaunty haircut grown out into something long and wild—she acted differently too. While she had formerly presided over us, she now hovered and retreated. Sometimes her eyes looked sleepy and vacant, at other times they lit up with a kind of furtive, wide-eyed astonishment that suggested she saw something we didn't. She accepted our offerings politely, like the good child she'd always been, and was glad as usual to be catered to, but she didn't seem to quite understand who we were.

She was already speaking in accents that weekend and saying things that didn't make sense. She switched without warning from baby talk to a Southern drawl to a kind of grandiose Pidgin English that sounded like a bad imitation of some middle European baroness. Sometimes she shouted obscenities in a deep coarse voice. We asked her questions but the answers were weird, unsatisfying, and vague, not quite connected to what we wanted to know. And then there was the laughter. Without warning or provocation, in response to the blandest comment from one of us, she would erupt, hysterically, convulsively, in a kind of wracking, sobbing, shrieking hilarity that caused her to clutch at herself and then drop to her knees and crouch on the floor looking up at us with a stunned, embarrassed expression that seemed to say, "Can you believe it? Can you believe this is happening?"

Could we believe what, though? We didn't have the slightest idea what was happening. It was as if she'd been possessed by a demon, put under a spell.

I went back to school at the end of the weekend, and two weeks later, Barb and Karim came to Champaign to visit me at my first apartment. I had no way of knowing this would be my first and last chance to entertain my sister in my own home and it bothers me now that I can't remember what I cooked or even if I did. I do remember that we went out one night to a bar I liked and that the three of us shared a pitcher of beer. It was almost like old times, when I'd visited them in Lexington, except that now the old intensity was gone, the old Barb was gone. She had nothing to say. We went to the university swimming pool on Sunday morning, and the three of us lay quietly in a row in the sun. When Barb lit a cigarette the lifeguard politely asked her to put it out and, instead of flirting and charming him into letting her finish, she just did as she was told. Barb didn't seem unhappy, she just wasn't there.

Then they left, and my complicated life resumed. Somehow I got through that semester and all the ones that followed, but for the rest of my college years, school hardly kept my attention. It all suddenly seemed like ridiculous fluff compared to the strange and distracting developments in my family.

At the end of the summer, Karim rented a car and drove to Lexington to see old friends and check up on his research and also, I think, to take a break from us. While he was gone, my parents and Barb and I drove to Door County, Wisconsin, to stay a few days at an old lakeside hotel we'd been going to for years.

My father booked two rooms—Barb and I were to share. When we arrived, he took me aside and gave me an assignment. He told me to get Barb to talk about what had happened "over there." So between visits to the beach and after sedate family suppers in the rustic dining room, Barb and I sat chain-smoking side by side in our tiny room on the matching chenille spreads that covered our girlish twin beds. We'd never shared a room before, and it felt strangely intimate as I tried to engage her in conversation by telling her things about me. Though I was nineteen to her thirty, I talked about sex. I figured it was my best shot to keep her interest. I told her about my boyfriend Mike. She nodded and blew smoke rings. I told her about the man in the room across the hall who was watching us, who'd stood in the doorway, waiting for me to walk by, with his swimming trunks down around his pale, round thighs. I tried to make it funny, and when she laughed her wracking, sobbing laugh, I thought I was getting somewhere. I was trying to re-create our old intimacy, trying to inspire solidarity, I suppose—a cozy girls-against-the-boys atmosphere that would encourage her to confide in me all the terrible things we imagined had happened to her, things we supposed were sexual though none of us ever said so. But it didn't work. She seemed to like my stories but she had nothing to say on the subject. I felt like a snoop and that I'd failed my assignment. We talked and smoked, like in the old days, but what little she said did nothing to explain her condition.

Later, my father used his own techniques and tried to get her drunk to make her talk, but that didn't work either. We all assumed she was keeping a terrible secret. Only much later did it occur to me that maybe she wasn't, that maybe she didn't know what had happened to her any better than we did.

Back then, except for her wild laughter and occasional obscene outbursts, Barb seemed passably normal as long as you didn't look too deeply into her eyes. She was thirty years old that summer, beautiful in her thin, startled-looking way, and in her black bathing suit and big sunglasses, stretched out on the pier with a magazine in her lap, she attracted attention from men. I was supposed to be her keeper that summer, but I was more interested in being her protégé, and as she lay dreamily squinting off across the water, chain-smoking her Tareyton cigarettes and occasionally breaking into raucous laughter at nothing, I only pretended not to notice the attention we were attracting. She couldn't have cared less.

Chapter Five

By the end of the summer, when it was clear that Barb wasn't getting any better, an understanding was reached that she would stay with my parents while Karim returned to Iraq for the academic year. The decision was unanimous. Karim needed to get back to work and didn't see any prospect for recovering their old life together if she went with him in her current state. My parents weren't going to let her leave if they could help it. And Barb wanted to stay. Or at least she didn't want to leave. I think Karim's idea was that we would get her fixed somehow and return her to him at the end of the year a better Barbara, more like she'd been before. He'd spent the summer pleading with her to get help, waiting for her to change, and worrying that she wouldn't, his mood vacillating between lovelorn patience and barely suppressed anger. He wanted his wife back—by now, she hardly seemed to notice him—and if a year apart was what it took, he was willing to wait.

But she did not prove to be an easy fix. At first, my parents tried the path of least resistance, hoping that family and familiar surroundings would provide a safe zone in which Barb could get better on her own. They assumed trauma and held Karim—or at least his country and culture—responsible and thought that once he left, she would relax and start to recover. It wasn't a bad plan to start with, but when it didn't work, when in fact she seemed to get worse, they didn't know what to do next.

So Barb got worse, or appeared to. Maybe her symptoms just surfaced. Karim had been dosing both Barb and himself with lithium to quell what he called their nerves. Without the tranquilizer to mask her symptoms, Barb went from vacant, glazed, and sleepy to psychotic.

As my sister got louder, weirder, and less social, my parents' response was denial. They absorbed every bizarre scene as if it were normal. It wasn't so bad, they said. It could be worse. She wasn't burning down the house. They were solicitous of her few demands—cigarettes, candy, industrial-sized bottles of Chanel No. 5—and accommodated her increasingly odd behavior by overlooking it. It didn't help that Barb showed no interest in getting what we called well, that she in fact flatly denied having a problem. When my parents asked her how she felt, she said fine, and when they asked if she'd like to see a doctor, she said no.

They didn't press. Partly it was out of respect for my sister's privacy. But it was also what they wanted to hear, despite the fact that by then it was becoming clear that her problem lay beyond the healing powers of ice cream, long naps, and common sense. They needed to hear Barb was fine, because if she wasn't, that meant it was time to do the one thing they most dreaded—seek outside help.

For a long time afterward, I wondered how things would have turned out if Barb had gotten help then. In those days, she still left the house. Maybe she could have been imposed upon to take some responsibility for her own care. Speedy intervention might have prevented her subsequent free fall. Though I see now that it also might have precipitated what my parents most feared, sidelining her differently, and more harshly, by shunting her into a life of hospitals, bad drugs, and bad drug side effects.

But we'll never know. My parents were both, if for different reasons, profoundly suspicious of doctors and hospitals. Their attitude bordered on negligence sometimes—I once stepped on a broken bottle in the lake, nearly severing a toe, and was treated by my mother with a Band-Aid and Mercurochrome—but I think their avoidance of professional help in my sister's case was more fear than indifference.

Despite my parents' ongoing war over almost everything else, here was one thing they could agree on. Doctors were to be avoided. By then, it had become part of our family culture, an assumption as unquestioned as turkey for Thanksgiving dinner. Not that they hadn't sought help from doctors over the years. They had. But when doctoring hadn't prevented the inevitable, which in my family included not only the usual human portion of pain, sickness, and death but also a disproportion of mental problems, they'd decided that if it couldn't be cured, why bother? They'd just tough it out.

My sister's spectacular meltdown must have seemed to my mother like just one more body blow in a lifetime of them. It had begun when she was a child, with her high-strung father's "nervous breakdowns." The only detail she offered was that he'd once become "upset" during a particularly noisy fireworks display. It's hard to say now which came first—the collapse of his law practice and subsequent bankruptcy in the midst of the Depression, his erratic behavior, his marital troubles, or his mental problems—but the cumulative effect was hard on his young family, and the electroshock therapy he received during his various stays at the Milwaukee Sanitarium and Manteno State Hospital neither cured him of his moods nor restored family stability.

My mother always seemed poised for the next disaster, and her prolonged despair after her mother's suicide wasn't even her first or her worst. It was understood in our family, if seldom discussed, that she suffered from very dark moods—her terrors and tempers were the secret my childhood bravado attempted to conceal—and that the most terrifying manifestation had been her depression after the birth of my brother.

She discussed it with me only once. During the worst of it she "saw things," she said, but refused to say more. What few additional hushed references she'd made over the years made it sound like a textbook case of what's now called postpartum psychosis, a rare but real condition triggered by a drop in estrogen that causes hallucinations and sometimes leads to infanticide and suicide. In 1946, though, her condition was considered more psychological than chemical, if not just bad character. After all, what kind of a woman can't take care of her own newborn baby?

This experience—and the failure of the medical and psychiatric community to treat it successfully—scared and alienated both my parents. As my mother got older, she grew increasingly, fiercely afraid of doctors and the bad news she expected them to give her. By the time she was in her fifties, when Barb came home from Iraq, she'd resigned herself to living with whatever problems she had rather than submitting to the greater suffering of trying to fix them. Her last consensual meeting with anyone remotely medical was a trip to the dentist that ended when she jumped out of the chair and ran away.

My robustly healthy father was suspicious of the medical profession for his own reasons, perhaps the main one being just contrariness. He'd inherited a do-it-yourself mind-set from his pioneer-stock ancestors, and the idea of some authority knowing more than he did about the workings of his body or his mind insulted his sense of rugged individualism.

One of his favorite stories was about his mother, who fell ill with a fever while giving birth to her youngest child in the newly built town hospital after successfully having her first three at home. This was 1918, the year half a million Americans died in a flu epidemic—no visitors were allowed. My grandfather, unimpressed with preventive hygiene and determined to see his wife, scaled the hospital wall and climbed through her window, arriving just in time for her to dictate the recipe for a curative poultice. My grandmother recovered, and my father triumphantly concluded that his parents' contempt for petty rules and conventional medicine had saved his mother's life.

Of my father's many yarns, this was one of his favorites, especially as he got older, and although it is a fantastically good family story, hinging as it does on my grandparents' superpowers—wall-scaling, magical healing—I wonder whether it is in fact completely true. Once my father got going on a story, he was prone to cast a spell not only over his audience but also over his own memory. Forced to choose between the literal and the literary, he often chose the latter. Embellished or not, though, the story proved one of his deepest beliefs, that self-reliance trumps medicine every time.

So when it came to Barb, neither of my parents held much hope for the medical possibilities available to them. After they'd asked if she wanted to talk to someone about how she felt and she said no, the project lagged. How could they argue when they felt exactly the same way?

In the meantime, my sister was getting visibly, audibly worse. We began to hear her in her bedroom or standing on the stair landing engaged in loud arguments with parties we couldn't see, delivering foul-mouthed monologues that sounded like a news correspondent with a microphone in her ear reporting from hell. The content of these reports concerned murder, mayhem, rape, torture, and gas attacks but the plots were hard to follow.

"They're trying to kill me," she often said. She seemed to speak not to us—if we interrupted, she looked startled—but to a third party to whom she described diabolic conversations and activities of a crowd of invisible others, as if she were narrating a riot or an unruly debate. She gave the characters she reported on bizarre or whimsical names—one of her regulars was Two Tom T, a poetic confluence of our father and brother, both of whom were Toms. She made up quasi-scientific words, marched up and down the stairs dozens of times a day sometimes shouting sometimes mumbling in accents. Many of her sentences began with "Now they're telling me ... " but if we asked her who exactly was telling her, she wouldn't answer—and if we asked her if she heard voices, she said no. She stopped calling my parents Mom and Dad and started to refer to them as she and he or the old woman and the old man. Later she just called my father Hawkins.

On warm days these monologues moved outdoors where Barb would lie on her back in the grass smoking, no longer bothering with a lawn chair. The streams of smoke and mumbling and occasional foul language that rose up out of the grass must have alarmed the neighbors, though they liked my parents and never complained.

Later these broadcasts would become even more intense and continuous, but in those days, they were sporadic and Barb interrupted them to interact with us as if switching channels, becoming polite and social, almost her old self as she sat down at the ancient card table to join in on the occasional family Parcheesi game. In those days, she still could be coaxed out of the house. She even came along on outings to restaurants sometimes, though her strange behavior made this increasingly difficult. Sometimes my mother took her on walks around town to do errands.

My mother liked the company. She'd been home alone and lonely since I'd left for college, and she cheerfully overlooked Barb's odd behavior at first—even seemed to enjoy it, egg it on. Once, as they'd passed between two churches on a walk through their sedate suburb, Barb had shouted obscenities, and my mother, an anarchist at heart and a dedicated non-churchgoer, laughed about it later in the telling. Something about my sister's wildly expressive derangement pleased her.

If my father's sense of social decorum was challenged to the edge of capacity by my sister's behavior—and this was to be only the beginning; the trial would go way, way further—my mother, though later assuming a kind of guilty sorrow over it, early on seemed to just enjoy having my newly unhinged sister around. For one thing, she was relieved. She'd been having dreams while Barb was in Iraq that warned her of trouble. And though my mother and sister had often been at odds when Barb was younger, now that she was back, and ill, they seemed to be newly attuned to one another, similarly off the grid of conventional behavior, if for different reasons.

They became constant companions, their days bracketed by my father's comings and goings. His presence, at night and on weekends, lent a certain dynamic tension to the household that required attention to his opinions and the preparation and consumption of large amounts of food at regular intervals. While he was gone, they could float.

There was a period when they entertained the daily visitations of a neighborhood cat that arrived on the porch every morning after my father left for work and was invited in by my mother, who fed and doted on him. Then the cat would flow upstairs and settle himself luxuriously in a slanted spot of sun on the bed in the room across from my sister's. I remember being home on a school break and watching the cat lounge territorially across the chenille spread as my mother and sister fluttered about him like ladies of the harem attending to a small, fat sultan. I was struck by how alike they were. At that moment they seemed happy, and their attentions to that cat came to represent for me the delicate balance of their relationship outside the purview of my father, who did not like cats.

I was a painting major in those days. Most of my work was assigned—still life, figures, design exercises—but in my junior year I took an independent study and made a painting depicting two women, entwined. I painted them in shadow, in different shades of red, wearing hooded garments that now seem to me like burkas, with their silhouettes blended together so that one contour flowed into the other. I intended it as a portrait of my mother and sister as one person, the physical blending of their two faces a clumsy symbol of what I'd later learn was called codependency.

But the intertwining of their lives was more than that too. This thing they shared, this extreme otherworldliness, seemed to me like a kind of legacy, a self-destructive destiny passed down through my family's feminine lineage from my maternal grandmother to my mother to my sister. I worried I was next.

It was hard to concentrate on school, hard to sleep, hard to get up in the morning, hard to be around people, sometimes even hard to be with Mike, though he did everything he could to make it easy. I made him promise we wouldn't get married. To me, marriage and maternity equal madness.

I felt I had to do something to fix my family. In the autumn after Barb's return, I went to the university health clinic and made an appointment with a psychiatrist—to get help for Barb, that is, not for myself, and also, I think, to prove my parents wrong for not taking action. I wanted to set them straight or at least force them to do something so I could get on with my own life. Instead, after I told my story, the psychiatrist asked about me. I must have been an open book of trouble, and here was my chance to get help, but that wasn't what I was there for, and when the doctor said he couldn't help my sister but maybe he could help me, I left, angry and disappointed.

It was a missed opportunity. I see that now, but it hadn't occurred to me yet how wrapped up my life was with Barb's. It hadn't occurred to me that dealing with how I felt about her and my family and the barely contained anxiety, not to mention anger, I was carrying and would carry for the next thirty-three years in anticipation of inheriting responsibility for her, would help us both. I just felt it was my lot in life to fix hers or wait until someone else did and that then and only then could I attend to my own. It was to be a long wait.

Chapter Six

Karim stayed in contact for the nine months he was away. He wrote pleading letters to all of us and particularly to Barb in his stilted, expressive English and, on Barb's birthday, sent a dozen roses, which appeared on the front porch just as they had in the days before he and Barb were married. Barb, though, seemed uninterested. She was indifferent to the flowers and left his letters lying around the house like junk mail.

When Barb didn't write back, Karim began to write to my father, who saved his letters in a dingy manila folder in a businesslike place between car titles and tax returns, far away from the softer, secret spot he'd stashed my sister's letters.

Karim sounds plaintive, frustrated, exhausted. "My life in Iraq without Barb is very hard," he says. "I hate everything over here." He complains that Barb never writes to him and that she is not trying to get better. He complains that his work is tedious, says he is lonely and worried and can't sleep and wonders why Barb hasn't gotten a job. He writes:

I don't understand why Barb does not want a job in downtown and permanent. This will keep her busy and she needs it very much. I am very worried about Barb, I have heard nothing from her the past three weeks.

I hope she is in good health. Please Dad write me more about her health. I think about this constantly.

This complaint, that Barb wouldn't take a job, though wildly out of sync with how sick she was by then, is telling and oddly touching. Instead of reverting to the stereotyped overbearing Middle Eastern patriarch we'd all imagined Karim was on the verge of becoming, one who wanted to keep his wife contained, controlled, and out of sight in a small dark room—which in fact is what ended up happening to my sister in the United States—Karim was brokenhearted that Barb was no longer the ambitious, passionate, independent-minded American girl he'd married.

This conversation in letters between Karim and my father appears to have continued throughout the year, though little evidence of my father's side of it remains except for Karim's increasingly frustrated replies. Why hadn't Barb written, he wanted to know. What was she doing? Had she gotten a job yet? Had she seen a doctor? What was going on over there? The sense in Karim's letters is that my father had gone silent on the subject, probably because there was no progress to report.

Finally, in May of 1975, as Karim's spring semester drew to a close, he wrote to say he'd begun making plans to visit for the second summer. Gone by now was the lovelorn tone of his earlier letters. A new impatience had crept into his voice.

I am very disgust [crossed out] unpleased with Barb's performance. Not only not writing but also not admitting the reality that she is not normal and must see some doctor. I really think she is happy the way she is but the question is, how about the other part of the story—me, Karim. I really don't like this and I really have to think about it. Do you believe that a person who likes to stay home doing almost nothing is normal? So, what "normal person" means is not our question but how to get Barbara as she used to be is the question.

······◆······

In June 1975, almost exactly one year after Barb and Karim first arrived home, Karim returned for the second summer.

From the beginning, things were tense. The early tender concern for Barb we'd all shared the summer before was now splintered and polarized. Now everyone was tired of the situation, uncertain of the future, frustrated with Barb and angry at each other. My family, especially my father, was angry with Karim, who seemed like as good a target as any to blame for the inexplicable changes in Barb. Her disconnected monologues about rape and torture, which we still thought might be reports of real events, had gotten worse instead of better. Karim was angry with us for not pressuring Barb to get help while he was away. My parents, as usual, were angry with each other about everything, and my father and I were at odds even more than before—I was openly critical of my parents' inaction. And everyone was angry with Barb for not wanting to get better.

My memory of that summer is a blur of hurt feelings and simmering tempers. I expressed mine by siding with the underdog and becoming Karim's confidante, thereby further enraging my father. That was only when I was there, though. Once again, I'd gotten a job on campus and signed up for a load of classes, commuting back and forth for family events but making a point of spending most of the summer away. By then I was living with Mike, a secret I shared only with Karim, though what I did hardly mattered by then. Barb's problems trumped everything.

The summer dragged on, holding us all in its chokehold of 90-degree temperatures, pollen and sweat, the heavy un-air-conditioned atmosphere in the house smothering us all with an ominous humidity that hinted at even-worse possibilities if only we could cool off enough to collect our thoughts and recognize them. As Barb increasingly refused to have anything to do with Karim, he, already nervous by nature, attempted to escape the tension by confiding in me, dosing himself with lithium, a supply of which he'd brought with him, and driving back and forth to Kentucky whenever he got the chance. His absences only infuriated my father more. My mother withdrew from us all, swooning and suffering from the heat and her allergies as she did every summer. Meanwhile, my brother arrived from North Carolina in the midst of all this, freshly in love and accompanied by his girlfriend, Anna, who met us all at what surely was our very darkest collective moment.

As July became August and August got hotter, the family tensions finally boiled over in a series of three disasters. The first was an accident. Karim totaled my father's car. My father's adored and adorable 1968 baby blue Volkswagen Beetle, the first new car he'd ever owned, was creamed, DOA. For years my father had had the use of a company Cadillac Fleetwood too—the car my mother liked to drive that had an automatic transmission, plush upholstery, air conditioning, electric windows, and the sleek black lines of a hearse—but the spartan gas-sipping VW with its hard seats and choppy manual transmission was my ever-contrary father's darling. He'd babied that car for years, driving it onto the lawn every Saturday morning and parking it hose-length away from the back door, spraying it down like an overheated pet pony.

Karim, always a nervous driver and at his worst that summer, had gone shopping, and while waiting to make a left turn off Milwaukee Avenue into the Golf Mill Mall, he was sideswiped by a speeding Buick Electra. It was a dangerous spot to make a turn—my mother had the only accident of her life in exactly the same place fifteen years later—and no one blamed Karim, not out loud at least. But it was the end of an era. It was the end of our family's experiment in optimism, the end of the romance Karim had shared with all things American, and most of all it was the beginning of the end of the goodwill we'd so carefully extended to each other over the years—the end of the hopeful, tentative, but sometimes very sweet relationship we'd had with Karim.

He wasn't badly injured, just further demoralized, but his head was bruised and bloody. I think he was allowed a few aspirin, though of course there was to be no doctor, and the next day when I needed to be delivered to the train to go back to school, he said he had a headache and opted to stay home from what would otherwise have been a group outing. As usual, tempers ran high whenever anyone was leaving the house, and a family argument broke out around who would stay home and who would go, though there was plenty of room in the Caddy for all. My sister wanted to come along, and this made my father erupt—at her, remarkably, since my mother and I were the usual objects of his wrath—shouting that her husband had a head injury and that she should stay home with him.

It was a memorable moment. First, that my father would recognize and sympathize with the physical suffering of anyone in the house was unusual enough. Even more remarkable, though, was the reshuffling of allegiances as my father expressed sympathy for Karim who, lying on the couch with a bloody towel on his head, inspired no sympathy in his wife. The moment passed—it was too late to achieve a repaired alliance between the men—but it signified my father's growing but, until now, unspoken frustration with my sister which, after he admitted it that day, would characterize their relationship from then on.

I don't remember who finally went and who stayed, only that I was desperate to get on that train and out of town. I was in a hurry to get back to my quiet domestic life with Mike, who grew organic tomatoes, baked bread from recipes in his Tassajara vegetarian cookbook, and was teaching me how to drive his green pickup truck. And, oh yes, my classes—whatever those were about.

Things unraveled fast after that, and by the end of August, Karim was making plans to leave again. I remember sitting on the back porch with him one afternoon sipping iced tea as he proudly showed me pictures of his graduate students, various group shots of young, smiling Iraqi boys and a few girls. He seemed happier and more relaxed than he had been all summer, and I realized that this faraway place in the photos he was about to return to was his real life now, not our messy family—no member of which except me, who at twenty hardly counted, would even speak to him civilly anymore. As much as he complained about the tedium of academic life, he wanted to get back to his students as much as I wanted to get back to Mike and our safe little apartment in Champaign.

It bothers me that I've forgotten the last time I saw Karim, but I do remember the last time we spoke. He promised he would call me from the airport in New York. It was long before the days of cell phones or even answering machines, and I stayed home that afternoon to be ready to pick up the black rotary dial phone in the hall, the only one we had, at the appointed time. Our conversation was brief and inconsequential—only later did I realize he'd called to say goodbye.

A few days later, the second disaster of the summer struck in the form of a letter from Karim, two handwritten copies of which were delivered to the house in separate envelopes, one addressed to Barb, the other to my father.

Neatly printed in Karim's precise handwriting and covering three pages of yellow legal paper, the letter rambles from anguish to argument to analysis. It contains protestations of love, promises of lifelong friendship, accusations of abandonment, descriptions of the physical symptoms of his distress, and quotations of Barb's exact words of resistance to his many efforts to get her to see a doctor both in the States and in Iraq. There's an itemized list of suggestions he'd made, including joint psychiatric help and an offer to resign from the university and move back to the States, all of which she'd rebuffed, references to their "six years of beautiful married life" and a review of the two and a half subsequent years of her unraveling. It ends, inevitably, with his first mention of what in my family was nearly unmentionable. Divorce.

It couldn't have been a surprise, but it must have been a shock. Not to Barb, who as usual didn't seem to care, but to my father. Who disapproved. Of divorce. And not just Barb's divorce but any divorce. It wasn't done in nice families; it wasn't even discussed, at least by him, though my mother slung the term around now and then. No matter how unhappy or sick or impossible or outgrown or ill suited or ill conceived or wrong headed or soul-sucking a marriage was, it simply had to continue, until death, as far as my father was concerned, not out of hope for reconciliation—my father was not a hopeful man at this point in his life—but as punishment for having failed.

My parents' response to Karim's letter was surprisingly prompt and energetic. Shocked into action after more than a year of nonintervention, they confronted Barb and somehow got her to agree to see a doctor. Within a week they'd made an appointment with a psychiatrist, and when Barb backed out of that, they negotiated a compromise. She would see the so-called family doctor for a routine checkup, though there was nothing routine about any of this.

The day before the exam my father called the doctor to explain the situation and outline his plan for how he wanted him to deal with it. His plan was that they—my parents and sister—would go for the appointment together. After examining Barb privately and presumably finding her physically well, the doctor would recommend to her in my parents' presence that she go to the hospital for tests for some made-up cause. Once there, my father reasoned, she could be seen by a psychiatrist.

So off they went. The doctor examined Barb, found her well, and asked her how she felt. "Fine," she said. Asked her if she wanted to go to the hospital for psychiatric testing. "No," she said. And that was that. No recommendation for further testing, no collaboration with my father's scheme.

My father was livid. As he saw it, this was their one and only chance to get Barb help and the doctor had blown it. He'd expected the doctor to go along with his plan, follow his orders, and when he hadn't, my father felt insulted and betrayed.

I wonder now what happened. I wonder whether the doctor changed his mind or just forgot my father's proposed scheme. Or had he rejected it out of hand, and if so, why? Was he put off by my father's imperiousness, or did he think the plan was unethical, deceptive? And if that was it, why hadn't he just said so? But whatever happened, my father believed he'd been lied to—he claimed the doctor had agreed to the plan—and what might have been a setback in another family was, for us, the end of the road.

But at least Karim's letter had shocked my parents into thinking about the future. And that meant thinking about money. If Barb wasn't going to move back into her old life, or out into some new one, and if Karim indeed intended to divorce her, there was the matter of her financial support to consider. Within days of receiving Karim's letter, my father wrote him back.

His letter—my father had started saving copies of his own letters by then—is formal, cool, and businesslike, especially in contrast to Karim's heated prose. By now all remnants of their old joshing relationship were gone—all those dinners at Matty's Wayside Inn, the outdoor concerts at Ravinia, the holiday martini-fests, the backyard barbeques, all gone. Now they were fencing about money.

"I am sure you will understand and agree that you should at this time set up a plan for your regular contribution to Barb's support and maintenance," my father wrote. "Please let me know if I can be of help in such planning. If in the longer term, we can get Barb back on her feet and working, such a plan would not be quite such an important factor to all concerned. As of now the responsibility lies not only with Mom and me, but ultimately with Tom and Margy as well."

· · · ◆ · · ·

The third blow in that summer's series of disasters fell shortly after I went back to school for my senior year. My parents called me the week before classes started to tell me that my father—distraught, distracted, drinking too much, and squeezed out by nepotism—had lost his job. He was fifty-eight.

Chapter Seven

Over the next year, Barb reached a plateau. She seemed to feel safest upstairs in her room where she could carry on uninterrupted conversations with her voices, but downstairs she allowed herself to be drawn into family activities as long as we didn't ask her about Iraq. When we did, she turned evasive and fudged the details like a cagey student answering a test question she didn't know the answer to.

In spring of 1976 my brother announced that he and Anna were getting married, and in October my family headed to Kinston, North Carolina, for the wedding. I had my first full-time job by then so I flew down for the weekend. My parents—with time on their hands, not wanting to risk a failed attempt to get my sister on a plane, and to accommodate my mother's fear of flying—drove to North Carolina from Chicago in their stripped-down, un-air-conditioned, radio-less Ford Pinto, the grimly pragmatic, unloved and unlovable replacement for my father's dearly departed VW.

My father was a tense, slow, and deliberate driver; the trip took them over a week. Somehow Barb held up, not only for the 2,000-mile road trip portion, cooped up in the Pinto, sharing restaurant meals and motel rooms with my parents, but also for three days of intense and continuous Southern hospitality culminating in a country club reception. The wedding itself—big, formal, Episcopal—posed the greatest problem. What if Barb erupted somehow? The solution was to assign Barb and me seats in the back of the church. I was instructed to escort her out in case she had a laughing fit. She didn't, though, not then or anytime that weekend, seeming to draw on her once formidable social skills to manage three days of nearly continuous contact with people she'd never met.

If Barb got worse that year, she did so in mostly subtle ways that were easy to ignore if you wanted to. She spent more time alone in her room. She began to eat her meals there, standing up, after loading a plate in the kitchen from the roasts and casseroles my unemployed father spent his days preparing. By then she'd moved into my brother's old bedroom, a small dark dormered boy's paradise, with a narrow single bed, raw pine walls, dark mahogany furniture from my father's own boyhood, model guns bolted to the wall, and a giant plastic bee my brother had built from a kit when he was twelve suspended over the bed. It seemed like a strange place for a grown woman with a troubled mind to make her own, but she didn't seem to notice and didn't change a thing except to take down the bee. She put a few, fastidiously folded articles of clothing in the dresser, hung a few more in the closet, stacked a few empty notebooks on the old oilcloth-covered table that served as a desk, and left it at that. She was home.

Then, in February of 1977, eighteen months after any of us had last seen or heard from Karim, two nearly identical letters arrived at the house, addressed respectively to my parents and my sister. A third had been sent to my Aunt Betty and Uncle Carl in Des Moines. The letters were from Karim. They announced he was divorcing my sister.

Each letter is slightly different—Betty and Carl immediately sent theirs to my parents—but they all say the same thing. After promising eternal friendship and love, Karim restates his case. Barb has no interest in getting well, refuses treatment, has no feeling left for him, and refuses to communicate. After observing that "we are getting older with time and one must think about his life," Karim says he contacted lawyers in Basra and Chicago to begin divorce proceedings.

"This step needs a better understanding from Mom and Dad," he writes to Betty and Carl. "They must know that Barbara has no feeling or affection for me. Margy knows everything. I told her these things two summers ago. So what use is married life without love and affection? I know they are considering this step but I pray that this [does] not hurt them. They are very good people and I will never forget them and we will stay friends forever."

My father was beyond furious. Karim hadn't even replied to his letter about Barb's financial support let alone come up with any money. Now, not only was he divorcing her, he'd broadcast the bad news to my mother's sister Betty and her husband Carl. Though they were among the few people outside the immediate family who knew about my sister's condition—they'd visited and seen for themselves— and although Betty was a psychologist and might be able to help, my father felt betrayed that Karim had included them in what he believed was a very private matter.

My father's sense of privacy and pride, though, was hard to distinguish from secrecy. And it wasn't just my mother's family that my father wanted to exclude; it was everyone. Much later we learned he'd never told his own sister what had happened either. What my father saw as an offense, though, Karim might have intended as a favor. Karim's understanding of family, both personally and culturally, encompassed a larger circle. If there was a nasty tinge of politics in his writing to Betty and Carl, of seeking support and approval from other, less-invested parties to get them to side against the tragic monolith my father had made himself into, he also seemed sincere when he said he hoped they could help soften the news. But these nuances were lost on my father, whose outrage knew no bounds. As far as he was concerned, from now on he could trust no one.

His response was swift, cold, and condescending. Ignoring Karim's pleas for love and friendship, my father lectures him on the meaning of his marriage vows—"I refer in particular to the obligation, which you accepted before God, family and community, to take care of her come what may, including sickness. I believe we agree she has a sickness"—scolds him for confiding in me, lectures him some more on what he assumes would be his response to being lectured, and then, getting down to business, argues for settling things without lawyers. The letter reads like a sermon.

What my father did not include, here or in any other letter I saw, was any acknowledgment of how difficult this was for Karim. Probably Karim's overwrought prose style didn't help. "I'm always biting my nails and burning inside," he wrote. Nothing could have alienated my father more. That Karim's situation bore a certain eerie resemblance to his own thirty years earlier, during my mother's worst depression, probably didn't help his case either. As far as my father was concerned, he'd toughed it out and now so should Karim.

Whether my father ever considered the possibility that a softer approach might at least have helped with financial negotiations, I'll never know. All I know is that Karim never wrote back. There would be no plan for Barbara's care or for anything else. That was the last communication that passed between them. From then on, everything was handled by lawyers.

· · · ◆ · · ·

The story went in those days that all a man had to do to get an Iraqi divorce was to proclaim "I divorce thee" three times and it was a done deal. Not so, though, if it involved an American citizen, at least if the divorce was to be valid in the United States. The next month my sister received a short letter from an Iraqi lawyer, in Arabic. My father sent it to a professional translator and six weeks later got it back in

English. The letter was a summons to appear in a Basra court on May 21, 1977. By then the court date was less than three weeks away. If some representative or member of the family had hoped to travel to Basra to attend the proceedings, it was now too late to arrange such a trip.

So the next time my sister received an official-looking letter from Iraq, my father took it to his friend Nick, the Syrian who ran the Edison Park liquor store where my father stocked up on his ever-expanding supply of jug wine and martini fixings. Who knows what nuances of legalese he sacrificed in return for this quicker, cheaper, friendlier method of translation but, according to Nick, the second letter notified Barb she was to appear in court on August 11, 1977, at 8:00 a.m. in Basra, Iraq, for final divorce proceedings.

I try to reconstruct that summer in my memory, try to think where I was or what I was doing that day my sister got divorced. It was a Thursday. Jimmy Carter was president. Was I working at my job selling thermal windows by phone? Or was I at Comiskey Park at a White Sox game, not with Mike—I'd broken up with him by then—but with my new boyfriend, Jeff? It's possible—they played the Cleveland Indians at home that day and lost, 3–1. Or was I packing for graduate school? What was my sister doing that day?

Whatever it was, the day came and went unmarked by either of us—though I suspect not by my parents—and on October 7, 1977, one last letter arrived, requesting that my sister sign, notarize, and return enclosed court papers to finish the proceedings. After almost eleven years of marriage, Barb and Karim were officially divorced.

What was missing from this legal correspondence was any mention of, let alone negotiation over, Barb and Karim's joint finances, the last reference to which was my father's sermonizing letter. After that, embittered and outraged, my father apparently gave up hope for ongoing support. Karim had left a modest amount of money in a bank account in the United States for Barb's use during their separation, but whatever else they'd accumulated together during their marriage remained his, including any saved income from her various jobs, overseas bank accounts, their car, house, and furniture as well as her clothes, jewelry, books, photographs, and any other personal belongings—my paintings!—she'd left behind. All my sister kept from her marriage was what she'd brought back in her suitcase on that trip home in 1974.

Chapter Eight

In July of 1977, while the divorce was underway, my parents made one more attempt to get Barb help.

At my mother's request, her sister Betty put my parents in touch with a psychiatrist who was head of in-patient psychiatric treatment at a good hospital near my   parents' house. My father called to make the appointment. After hearing his concerns—my father wanted to arrange a meeting in a non-hospital setting—and because we were the family of a friend, the doctor agreed to see my sister at his home on a Saturday morning. The idea was to soften the experience for Barb, not scare her. My parents were afraid that if they took her to a hospital, she'd bolt. So on July 30, 1977, my parents drove with Barb to Kildeer, Illinois, a countrified suburb about thirty miles north, to meet with Dr. Benjamin Jacobs.

I can imagine the hot, tense, hour-long drive. I see my anxious, furious, terrified, already white-haired parents, sweating with dread in the July heat in their un-air-conditioned car, pulling up at the rambling country house of the successful psychiatrist, my mother grim and pale with deep, permanent creases gouged between her eyebrows, her mouth drawn into a slit, my father red-faced, sputtering, and suspicious. I imagine them climbing out of their little blue car, that uncomfortable, immaculate, self-abnegating Ford Pinto, which I picture parked at the curb at the end of a long, lushly landscaped driveway. My mother emerges from the back seat, where she took to riding sometime during my childhood in apparent silent protest against my father's front seat lectures, though they've never explained this odd arrangement to me. I imagine my wild-eyed, wild-haired sister crouchingly emerging from the back seat as well, dressed in one of the strange layered, cut-off, and sewn-short outfits she's taken to wearing, not yet knowing the real mission of this trip and believing they are paying a social visit to a friend of my aunt's.

I imagine them standing at the door of the psychiatrist's house feeling desperate, my father hoping and doubting and saying neither but instead issuing useless, insulting orders as my mother and sister hang back, helpless to defend themselves except through listlessness. Then the door opens and they are greeted by the successful psychiatrist or perhaps by his cool and beautiful wife and invited out of the sweaty July heat into the artificial chill of their cool and beautiful house, a chill which my mother envies and my father hates, and led down a broad, well-appointed hallway as the doctor turns and introduces himself to my sister in his euphonious voice, explaining that he is a doctor and would like to ask her some questions. This is news to her. Then they arrive at his office door, and he invites her to enter.

Barb refuses. She's on to him now. *No, I'll stand right here,* I can hear her say, small but stubborn and prepared to drop and run as she strikes a defensive pose against the wall. So, while she waits outside the open door, my parents sit across from the doctor and describe the problem to him, conscious that she is listening, and when they are done, the doctor says he does not believe she is susceptible to outpatient treatment. He recommends she be hospitalized.

"How would we get her there—" my father asks, and then, lowering his voice, knowing she is just outside the door, adds, ". . . against her wishes?"

"Just bring her in," the doctor says.

"And if she won't go?" my father counters, his voice rising.

"Just call the ambulance," the doctor says. "The unwilling

patients usually come along when the ambulance arrives." Noticing my father's stricken expression, the doctor adds, "What can you lose?"

I imagine this is the moment at which my father loses his temper, the moment when my mother's wounded, worried silence turns to a hurt scowl. I imagine this is when the doctor draws back in his chair and sneaks a look at his watch. He refuses to argue, and finally even my father can't think of anything else to say. I imagine the doctor now taking off his glasses and setting them down on his desk, politely but firmly signaling that there is nothing more to say, that it is time for my parents to leave, to stand up and walk out along with my sister, who joins them at the door, to make their way back down the long hallway, through the cool and beautiful house, out the front door, into the heat, and down the long driveway to their hot, hard vinyl-seated Ford Pinto, and go home. Which they do.

The next day my father writes a memorandum describing this encounter. He is at the lowest point in his life. He is out of work, fifty-nine years old, father to a thirty-three-year-old daughter who has no means of support other than him and who is by now carrying on loud daily arguments with invisible enemies. Though he has two other children, and a wife, my father has no one to turn to because he trusts no one.

So he writes his memo to himself. He tries to be precise, calm, reasonable. He describes the meeting, the doctor's recommendation, quotes the exchange about getting my sister to a hospital:

This presents a big problem with me. I think the possible trauma that Barby might experience from having strangers snatch her out of her home could be inestimable. What bothers me especially is that a doctor who wouldn't dream of prescribing for a patient without knowing all he can about her otherwise, would prescribe this initial potentially dangerous step without knowing the risk.

I don't get it. She could become a lot worse. That there are risks once she is in a hospital I think I can accept. But blind force and hope for the best in this situation looks wrong. (If someone were burning the house or cutting their wrists, certainly.)

Here I am with a very hard decision to make. I have overruled or moderated doctors and lawyers before and time has proven me right. As of now, I can't come up with an alternative, but there must be one.

It was not an unhopeful note to end on. It suggested he intended to keep trying. But he never did come up with an alternative, unless that's what he considered what he ended up doing—gutting it out. My parents had reached another dead end.

My father kept the torn-up, taped-back-together $50 invoice— it's not clear who tore it up or why, although in those days Barb was a great shredder of everything from mail to clothing—filed away next to his memo. On top is a dated note that indicates he waited a highly uncharacteristic two-and-a-half months to pay. Maybe he was toying with the idea of not paying, but in the end he just paid late, his only act of protest against what he considered cruel and useless advice.

My father of course turned this encounter into a story. It started out as a tale of disappointment and frustration, peppered with derision, but over the years it stewed into something darker and more bitter. Early on he told the story plainly, if angrily, to explain his pessimism over professional advice that recommended a course of action both my parents felt they could not in good conscience take. Later, as my father's fury ripened, he used it as a cautionary tale to bolster his position on the uselessness of doctors. Somewhere over the years, though, the meaning of this story, as my father understood it, began to obscure the facts until finally in old age he swore to shocked listeners that the psychiatrist had told him all he could do was to drive my sister out to the country and drop her off in a field.

Let it be noted here that my father remained in sound mind for his full eighty-nine-and-a-half years. Though physically incapacitated for a few weeks at the very end of his life, he followed international news, received and entertained guests, kept track of football scores, and oversaw his finances up until he lost consciousness. This altering of fact was not dementia. It was not even deception. This story that my father told himself and anyone else who would listen was the truth about his life as he'd come to believe it. It was paranoia made into myth, an invention that told a truer truth of feeling than mere fact could ever do. It was a horror story, a Grimm's fairy tale of abandonment and evil enchantment that combined my father's sense of having been abandoned by the medical establishment with the fear he felt at his own ambivalence about abandoning my sister, and maybe it was even wishful thinking. Finally, by exaggerating to evil proportions the advice he'd been given, he got himself off the hook for doing something he wasn't sure he should have, despite all his bluster. No one could blame him for refusing to abandon Barb in a field somewhere, but it was a lot less defensible to refuse to take her to a hospital. And it was all wrapped up in one showstopper of a story that wasn't a lie so much as a legend which, by the end of my father's life, he'd come to believe.

Chapter Nine

Someone once said that to understand a woman, you need to know her father. Certainly that's true of my sister. Our father was the one who made the decisions that determined the course of her life when she no longer could. If he'd been a different man, less devoted, more trusting, less dutiful, more humble, less stoic, richer, poorer, more sensitive, less sensitive, differently sensitive, it all might have turned out differently. But to explain my father's nature requires a split screen of the mind. There was not just one Dad. There were at least two, and they were opposites, the good dad and the bad dad, and for every memory I have of my father's anger and spite and stubbornness and pigheaded pride, there is an opposite one of tenderness, steadfastness, humor, and imagination. These memories do not blend into a single complex whole over time, though, as you might expect, but remain separate and discreet, unblendable, as if he contained two men packed uncomfortably into one. My memories of him come in warring pairs.

In one bad dad memory I am about nine. It's a hot summer Saturday, August probably, and we've gone to the beach—my parents, my brother, and I. We've brought a picnic. My father's brought drinks, beer, maybe something stronger, and he's in his cups. A policeman appears to tell him he can't drink on the beach. My father's reply is haughty, if slurred. His grandfather used to own this town; he feels entitled to do as he pleases here. He calls the officer Copper. We leave soon after. My mother is embarrassed. On the way home, we stop at the Open Pit Barbeque, a festive noisy place with picnic tables where it doesn't matter if you have sand on your bare feet or, for that matter, if you're a loud drunk. My brother and I order sweet smoky BBQ sandwiches on soft buns with french fries. My parents order drinks.

I announce I'm reading a biography of Helen Keller. My father launches into a dramatic rendition of a Helen Keller joke, all the rage in 1964, the punch line of which is a mean-spirited imitation of Keller's speech. I'm mortified, not because he's making a scene—it's not even the first one that day—but because he's making fun of my hero.

This memory sparks its opposite from a couple of years later. My class is putting on a production of Julius Caesar, and I am to play the part of Brutus. I have memorized my lines—"Not that I loved Caesar less, but that I loved Rome more!"—and I think I've figured out how to look like a man: I will wear my long blond hair in a French twist. But there is the matter of the costume, a toga. Our teacher, Mr. Dieter, who takes this all even more seriously than we do, gives each of us playing the part of a Patrician a roll of purple satin ribbon on Monday afternoon and tells us to take it home and have our mothers sew it along the edge of a white bed sheet by Friday. I am in a panic. My terrible secret is that my mother doesn't sew. I don't sew. My sister sews very well and is living at home, but I can't ask her to do it—she'd consider it beneath her. Desperate but embarrassed, I can't tell anyone. Finally, I take the roll of purple ribbon home on Thursday night and give it to my father, and he, after a day of trading bonds on LaSalle Street, hand sews the length of ribbon along the edge of a bed sheet. This is 1966. I am Brutus. I am grateful. Forever.

So when I think about my father and try to understand his role in my sister's life, I think of both these fathers, but I have trouble holding the thought of them at the same time. I veer between them. I think of the stubborn, angry man holding a lifelong grudge against the only body of experts that might have been able to help my sister—doctors, psychiatrists, psychologists, social workers—out of a conviction that they are all categorically wrongheaded, untrustworthy, insensitive, presumptuous, arrogant and, most of all, against him. It becomes a point of pride, this belief, one that he would have been insulted to be shown was wrong. Over the years his conviction sometimes seems to overshadow the cause—my sister—and the more people try to convince him he's wrong, at times infuriating him even further by suggesting the course of inaction he's chosen borders on neglect, the more he barricades himself against any dissenting opinion.

On the other hand, I think of the father who, for thirty-three years, first along with my mother and then, after her death, alone for ten years, takes care of my sister. He saves every extra dime. He shops, he cooks, he serves three meals a day, he celebrates her birthdays with gifts and cakes, he does the laundry, he runs her errands, though sometimes grudgingly, for luxury goods and odd requests. She wants a brand of shampoo that is no longer made, a special kind of underwear. He fumes and grumbles but then sets out to find it. I try to help him buy her clothes. "It's easier for me," I say. "Let me do it; I understand women's sizes." This is one thing I can absolutely do, but he hates it that the clothes I buy fit her better than the ones he buys. He not only wants to do it, he wants to be better at it than I am. He wants to do it all himself, hobbling clueless through department stores on his arthritic legs in his ninetieth year with a list of not-quite-right sizes and a measuring tape, his only weapons against the capricious women's clothing industry. My sister is so small that he usually comes home with children's clothes. Sometimes I sneak gifts to her, hiding them in my coat or bag when I visit, to avoid his angry outbursts and hurt feelings, to spare him the sorrow of my success in what he fails at—finding things to please her. It's hard to say whether he's angry because I am "spoiling her," as he often says, or because he feels I am outdoing him. "They're just clothes," I say. "Let me help." But he refuses. He makes it his life's work to find her these things or to die trying. He dies trying, but that's getting ahead of the story.

Chapter Ten

Thus began a long period of stasis. My parents adjusted to my sister's altered state by simply absorbing her into their routine. They didn't ask much—though my father tried to think of what he called "chores" for her, pressing her to re-sew the occasional fallen button—and things settled into a pattern that would remain constant for many years.

This reabsorption of Barb back into my parents' daily lives happened at just the moment when their last child, me, was leaving home. By the time my sister's divorce became official, I was gone, in graduate school. My father was sixty then, my mother fifty-six. My parents had already prolonged their caregiving years by an extra decade by having a late third child; now my sister's return would prolong it indefinitely.

There's a truism in the mental health community that says that troubled families focus on the sickest member, even welcoming the sickness, to avoid dealing with other problems. It's hard to say now what might have happened if my parents had been free then to examine their lives and make choices about what to do next. Who knows how their marriage would have developed if they'd found themselves alone together for the first time in over thirty years.

It was the late 1970s—what would have been my mother's empty nest coincided with the second wave of the women's movement. It might have been a window of opportunity for her, not to leave probably, but at least to spread her wings. She was calmer in middle age as she emerged from the sadness and anger and suffocating, confusing hormonal haze of her younger life. When I was in high school, she'd begun to take courses, written a couple of articles for the local paper, and found a part-time job she liked. If she'd felt freer, less encumbered by family and the cross-generational burden of mental illness, she might have kept going, begun to stand up to my father, who in turn might have begun to respect that. She might have staked a claim to her own independence, even to the point of shrugging off his constant criticism instead of buckling under it.

And my father, whose social appetite, energy, and work ethic, not to mention finances, probably wouldn't have allowed him to retire even if Barb hadn't come home, might instead have chosen to work part time—he'd gotten another job by then—rather than stay on full time until the age of seventy-five. My parents owned a few acres in Michigan, the last piece of a family farm that figured importantly in my father's nostalgic childhood stories. He'd fantasized to me about building a cabin there. Both my parents romanticized country life; I suspect they had ambitions in that direction they'd never mentioned to me. But neither of my parents felt they could entertain any of these possibilities as long as Barb was ill.

So my father went to work five days a week and to church on Sundays. My mother stayed home with Barb, as if my sister was a child who required constant care.

Barb's childlike status was reinforced by the fact that she no longer left the house. It was hard to tell if her refusal to leave was a response to my parents' last attempt to get her to a doctor or based on some other, less rational fear, but whatever it was rendered her completely dependent. Anything she wanted—from food to clothing to her beloved Tareyton cigarettes—she had to request from my parents. This last item was supplied by my father, who was in charge of stocking up on the household vices, until he quit smoking and decided that she should too. After that when Barb asked for cigarettes, my father told her to buy her own. Since she had no money and no intention of leaving the house, this effectively ended her habit, though not through any decision of hers.

She didn't protest, just relinquished this luxury as she had everything else in her life, without argument. By then her strongest feelings seemed not to be attachments but fears. She was afraid of the basement, so she did her laundry by hand in the bathroom sink. She wouldn't allow anyone to stand or walk behind her, withdrew when people came to the house, wouldn't sit at a table to eat with any member of the family, wouldn't allow herself to be touched, and would not—could not—leave the house, even for a ride to a drive-in restaurant.

Barb still had an occasional brush with the outside world, when it came to her, but these usually didn't go well. Jeff had spent the night at the house once early in our relationship, in the room across from Barb's, and reported waking up at daybreak to the disconcerting sound of her shouting, "He thinks he can rape any woman he wants!" I assured him later she hadn't meant him, but I wasn't usually around to interpret, and these encounters just served to isolate my family further, making my parents yet more afraid to let the world in.

Once an old high school friend of my sister's stopped by for a visit. Alarmed by Barb's behavior, she asked my parents if she was in treatment. The friend left abruptly, though, after an angry exchange with my father, who considered it none of her business. Another time, an eccentric acquaintance of mine called looking for my phone number. Barb answered the phone that night, one of the last times she did, and after a brief and bizarre conversation, handed the receiver to my father.

My father: Hello?

Doug: Well, your wife's a real snapper, isn't she?

Of course it became a family joke. Even funnier than Doug's mistaking my sister for my mother, who took pride in her careful elocution, was the fact that he'd felt free to comment so rudely on her manners. The comic absurdity of this event, though, belied the more painful truth my parents were learning. My sister's bizarre and sometimes antisocial behavior attracted unwanted attention from unsympathetic or just uncomprehending outsiders. It demanded either secrecy or some kind of explanation that left them open to insensitive interpretation and judgment. They opted for secrecy or at least an extreme form of self-containment that looked very much like shame.

···◆···

In the meantime, I'd finished graduate school and moved back to Chicago where I'd taken a part-time job at a medical library to supplement my meager teaching income. I worked nights shelving books and making photocopies, with plenty of downtime to browse the stacks. Soon I discovered Silvano Arieti's *Interpretation of Schizophrenia*. It had won the National Book Award a few years earlier and, by 1980, when I came across it, it was still the last word on the subject.

Barb had never been formally diagnosed, but everything I found in the book confirmed what we'd suspected, that she was schizophrenic. The bigger revelation, though, was that this condition, which in some ways seemed like such an oddly intimate expression of our family psychology, turned out to be a diagnosable disease with predictable symptoms. Another revelation was its frequency. Arieti cited the now familiar statistic of 1 in 100 and, as shockingly high as this number was, it was also reassuring. It meant we weren't alone.

Finding the book was like finding a key to a locked room. I wished I could share it with my parents, but I knew I couldn't. Although

Arieti didn't attribute the disease exclusively to family circumstances, he upheld the long-standing belief that "schizophrenogenic parents" caused or worsened it. This theory has since been discredited; schizophrenia is now known to be a heritable physical illness of the brain rather than a psychological condition brought about by trauma or bad parenting, but the bad parenting theory dominated both popular and scientific thinking at the time. The possibility that our family psychology was not the cause of Barb's problems but was in fact the result of them, or rather the result of similar problems in earlier generations with some version of her condition, was never discussed.

Because of Arieti's beliefs on schizophrenogenic parents, though, I never showed the book to my parents. I didn't want to hurt or anger them further—everything they'd learned about mental illness reinforced their feelings of guilt and responsibility. They'd begun to accept that Barb's problems were deeper than anything that could have resulted from her having lived in Iraq, and their expectation of condemnation from the outside world for having done something terribly wrong was yet another reason not to seek help for what didn't seem fixable anyway.

Something else happened that year to change my understanding of our situation. Maybe as a result of my reading or maybe because I was back in Chicago and newly immersed in the family drama or maybe just because I was sick of all the secrecy, I began talking about my sister with anyone who would listen, including the women I worked with in the library. We were a staff of nine, most of the others were professional librarians twice my age. Several had adult children and soon I learned something extraordinary. Two women on our staff had schizophrenic sons—two!

The odds were staggering. One third of our little cohort had a schizophrenic family member. And that didn't include a much whispered about fourth woman who kept to herself and had suicide-attempt scars up and down her arms. A fifth had a daughter with Down syndrome. I was learning that mental illness—no matter how quiet it was kept—was more commonplace than I'd ever dreamt.

Chapter Eleven

Although Barb wouldn't visit me, she liked it when I went to see her and seemed to like when I brought Jeff. We were living together by then and, despite our many ups and downs, he was unfailingly kind to my sister. It was partly her openness to him that gave my father his next idea.

By now it was 1983. My father was managing a computer lab at a community college, having reinvented himself in his mid-sixties after a very rough few years. A post-hippie looseness lingered on campuses in those days, especially at sleepy suburban community colleges. My father had grown his hair out a little, traded his business suits for khakis and a lumberjack shirt. He rode his bicycle to work now instead of taking the commuter train, and every morning he packed a brown bag of lovingly assembled leftovers—no more three-martini business lunches for him—and when weather permitted he'd picnic on the lawn with students. This job, and the friends he made there, was the best thing that had happened to him in a long time. Maybe that's why he felt free to speak openly of Barb, at least to one sympathetic colleague who suggested she might qualify for Social Security disability benefits.

This possibility both offered an opportunity and posed a problem. The opportunity was for a little more income. Barb had none, and even though my parents had paid off their house and despite my father's thirty-year career as a bond trader and financial consultant, they weren't especially well off. Getting some kind of aid for my sister would help them save for her uncertain future.

The problem was that Barb needed a diagnosis to qualify, which took us back to the original dilemma. She wouldn't go to see someone who could make that diagnosis. My parents couldn't or wouldn't make her go.

But, inspired this time by the prospect of financial help, my father set aside his distrust of the mental health profession long enough to find a social worker who agreed to make a house call—in those days social workers could present evidence of illness to a psychiatrist who then made a diagnosis without seeing the patient. The plan seemed perfect, except my father worried Barb might not cooperate.

Barb mostly recoiled from anyone outside the immediate family, but if she liked Jeff, my father reasoned, maybe she'd talk to some other young man too, as long as he was somehow connected with me. My father decided that the male social worker should pose as my date. I'd go for dinner at my parents' house, and afterward he'd show up and ask Barb questions. Never mind that he'd be carrying a clipboard and writing down her answers, never mind that Barb knew I already had a boyfriend.

It seems more than a little odd now. I understand that my parents didn't want to risk another rejection, but I also wonder if my father just couldn't resist the opportunity for a bit of improvised theater. He loved hoaxes, tricks, practical jokes. Maybe this was more of that.

Whatever the reason, we all went along with the ruse, even Bob, the social worker, who arrived at my parents' house after dinner one evening and pretended to be my friend long enough for me to invite my sister downstairs and introduce them. After some pleasantries, he proceeded to ask questions: What day of the week was it? Who was the president of the United States? What year was it? How old was she? How did she feel? Did she hear voices? She cooperated for a while, and then as the questions got harder and more personal, she became suspicious and coy. "Oh, you know the answer to that," she replied cagily, deflecting the questions back to Bob. Finally she retreated upstairs.

But Bob had heard enough. Barb was schizophrenic, he said; she should qualify for benefits. Then he packed up his clipboard and left, politely reserving any opinions he'd formed about the rest of us. Soon afterward he started paperwork that eventually resulted in Barb's receiving small but helpful monthly payments and which allowed my parents to be named my sister's legal guardians.

That my father was able to make these crucial arrangements with relative ease was, like so much of what he did in regard to my sister, both heartening and maddeningly not enough. When I took over her care twenty-four years later, the fact that she was already in the system made my job immeasurably easier than it would otherwise have been. I was grateful to my father for having set it up, to Bob for coming to the house, and to the Social Security system for the small but regular monthly checks that helped pay the bills over the years. But the ease with which this help was found begs a larger question. If a social worker had so willingly come to the house in 1983, and even been flexible enough to accommodate our little charade, what other help might have been forthcoming had my parents only asked?

Chapter Twelve

Schizophrenia is a cruel disease. The lives of those affected are often chronicles of constricted experiences, muted emotions, missed opportunities, unfulfilled expectations.

Surviving Schizophrenia: A Family Manual
—DR. E. FULLER TORREY

After my father died, my brother and I cleaned the den. It was the room I'd brought him home to, where I'd installed the hospital bed and rolled his ancient TV, on its rickety cart, to stand in front of the bookcase so he could watch the Chicago Bears as he departed his life. For fifteen days, as my father lived and died in that room, the sagging bookcase filled with and then disappeared under piles of medical supplies. Afterward, when we cleared them away, something bright yellow caught my eye. There, wedged between one last pile of rubber gloves and my father's twenty-eight-volume collection of the complete writings of Robert Louis Stevenson, was the 1985 paperback edition of *Surviving Schizophrenia: A Family Manual.*

I pulled it out and started to read. Though the book had been there twenty years and the paper was brown and brittle, the words on page two could have been written about my family that morning.

The stigma of schizophrenia makes it all the more tragic. Not only must persons affected and their families bear the disease itself, but they must bear the stigma of it as well. . . . The magnitude of schizophrenia as a national calamity is exceeded only by the magnitude of our ignorance in dealing with it. For it is only our ignorance which continues to keep schizophrenics in the closet.

Here is the book that could have and should have changed my family's life. Someone else must have thought so too. Someone gave this book to my parents, and it appears to have been someone in the profession—possibly my aunt, maybe one of my father's friends at the college. Tucked inside the front cover was a yellowed publicist's letter that accompanied what looks like a promotional desk copy. It invites readers to attend appearances by the author in major cities, including Chicago, and to set up family meetings with the doctor. Stapled to the letter is a two-page fact sheet summarizing Torrey's then-radical message. It is written plainly; any layperson could understand it. Schizophrenia is a brain disease that requires medical treatment, he says, "a real scientific and biological entity as clearly as diabetes, multiple sclerosis, and cancer are biological entities."

And below that, this crucial admission:

In the past it was believed that bad parenting, pathological family communications or even the patient him/herself was responsible for causing the disease. We now know that these things are not true. Meanwhile, however, a whole generation of schizophrenic parents and families has been made to feel guilty. Because of this, these parents and families are often very angry at mental health professionals.

Torrey lists symptoms—all observable in my sister—quotes extensively from patients who describe with alarming, eye-opening specificity their perceptions and hallucinations, and recommends drug treatment. He argues for kindness and destigmatization, and tells movingly of the shame and guilt families of schizophrenics suffer. The book is compassionate, practical, respectful of both patients and their families, written in plain English, and ends with an appendix of commitment laws by state and a state-by-state listing of family support groups. In short, it is exactly what my parents needed.

The earliest they could have seen this book was 1985, the year it was published, eleven years after my sister returned from Iraq. My parents would have been in their sixties. Maybe they felt it was too late for them to change. Barb, though, was forty-two.

I wonder now if my parents even read the book, which, though it didn't offer a cure, did offer hope for treatment in the form of medication and reassurance that they weren't alone or to blame. It also introduced an idea they hadn't appeared to consider at all: the healing value of community, the possibility of commiseration, comfort, insight, and information-sharing through association with other families with the same problem. This was an option they did not even discuss, at least with me. My parents weren't joiners, and even if they hadn't been lifetime experts at juggling their particularly toxic combination of secrecy, pride, and shame, I suspect they would have considered the notion of joining a family support group to be embarrassing and a bit like whining, something that was simply not for people like them.

But I don't know whether they read it or not. I only know that the book appeared in the house in the mid-eighties, first on the coffee table and then migrating to the bookshelf in the den where it remained. My parents didn't discuss it or press it on me, and I remember skimming it when it first appeared, but I didn't read it cover-to-cover either.

By that time, we were all tired of trying to figure out what to do. My own life had gotten increasingly complicated and was especially so that year. I'd suspended my campaign to help my sister in favor of trying to fix my own messy life. It was a campaign that seemed impossible anyway, since it depended entirely on my parents' cooperation.

And besides, that title—what a downer. *Surviving Schizophrenia.* Surviving, though it was what we were doing, sounded so desperate, so meager. It didn't come close to what we so irrationally but insistently wanted, which was not just survival or even a cure but a miraculous, spontaneous, and full recovery.

In those days I still regularly dreamed of exactly that. In my dreams—not fantasies but actual night dreams—my sister would call me on the phone or I would find myself sitting in a restaurant or walking down the street with her engaged in cogent, lively conversation. Always we were talking in my dreams, as we had when I'd visited her in Lexington, and afterward I'd wake up happy, basking in the glow of this incredibly good turn of events. Then I'd remember it was only a dream, and the rest of my day would be colored by a fresh sense of loss. I used to hope, even secretly believe, these dreams were prophetic, but now I know they were simply wishful thinking. I think we all felt that way—we all wished and secretly believed that one day the vibrant Barb who had gone missing from our lives would just show up and resume her old life. Anything less felt like a cheap substitute and wouldn't do. The book promised no such recovery, though, and we weren't ready to hear that; we weren't yet ready for the harder work of meeting her where she was.

So the book just sat there until I found it twenty-two years later, still on the shelf in the den where my father died. It wasn't news to me in January 2007 when I finally sat down to read it, but I wondered what it might have meant to my parents in 1985, if the little bit they may have read softened their life, if not my sister's, even a little. But I suspect it was another missed opportunity, another rescue boat that passed just out of sight, or one that came by too long after their course had been set. When I retrieved the book all those years later, the letter with its invitation was still tucked between the pages, suggesting maybe there was once a wish, a weak intention to seek help, lurking underneath my father's steely stoicism and my mother's sad, sighing resignation, and which, though never acted upon, hinted at hope for change. But in the end, the call was not made, the letter not written; things continued to continue as they had.

Chapter Thirteen

In 1992, my father retired from his job at the college. He was seventy-five and in most respects still going strong, though his arthritis was beginning to make it hard for him to walk the long hallways. That wasn't why he was retiring, though, he said. It was for my mother, whose health had begun to fail.

My mother, at seventy-one, was young by my father's standards, though not by her own. She'd already outlived her own mother and she felt tired, sad. Her heart hurt, her back hurt, and her most pressing physical problem—her failing eyesight—meant she couldn't drive, couldn't read and, increasingly, couldn't see us unless she stuck her face into ours and peered myopically as if looking into a dark room, a condition that just reinforced her sadness and isolation. We tried to talk her into going to an eye doctor, but of course that was out of the question. I went to Walgreen's and bought her a pile of ready-made glasses. She made a comedy of trying them all on and even picked out a pair and pretended they helped, to please me, but she never wore them. Whatever her problem was couldn't be cured so simply.

So my father retired, setting off a wave of change. Always a dominating presence in the house evenings and weekends, now he was there full time. My mother, who had done the shopping and, unenthusiastically, the cooking, at least on weekdays, for all those years, now couldn't see well enough to leave the house even for her weekly hair appointment at Art et Beauté without being escorted by my father. He took over—the house, the yard, the car, the shopping, everyone's lives. Most of all, he took over the kitchen.

Throughout my childhood he'd been in charge of Sunday and holiday dinners, usually roasts he put in the oven before he left for church, and for a few years he'd made wine out of everything from beets and dandelions to potatoes and Hawaiian punch. He'd always been an avid and imaginative cook, improvising ingredients and slugging down wine from a juice glass as he went along. Now he ruled the kitchen. It became his theater, his studio, his headquarters, his wheelhouse. He oversaw every detail of the groceries that went in and out, supervised leftovers as if they were troop supplies, and monitored every morsel of food consumed. "Look at her—she eats like a horse!" he'd bellow when my sister took seconds and thirds. To eat like a horse was a good thing, especially when my father was cooking.

He began making cakes, grinding his own sausage, baking apples and, at Christmas, candying ginger and grapefruit peel. He both catered to and tweaked the tastes of my mother and sister, who could ruin his day by rejecting his breaded eggplant.

What was a new and creative challenge for my father, though, was a further erosion of my sister's territory. Suddenly the quiet life she and my mother had shared, in which each respected the other's silences and eccentricities, disappeared as Barb became the focus of my father's scrutiny. If before she'd been free to wander the house uncommented on, at least by day, now her every move elicited an emotional, often critical, response. Her odd behaviors—in particular her long-standing habit of throwing useful things away—were on a collision course with his increasingly obsessive thrift. The more he tried to conserve, the more she slipped food into the garbage. For years, she'd done this with gifts of clothing, destroying a garment by cutting or ripping it before she threw it out so it couldn't be salvaged. I'd gotten used to it and considered waste part of the cost of shopping for her, but it drove my father crazy. He may have tried to tell himself it was the illness, but at heart he felt it was defiance and, worse, rejection of his hard-won Depression-era values. He took to scolding her as if she were a child, though by now she was in her fifties, and the kitchen became a battleground as my father patrolled the wastebasket, watching for discarded food or the occasional sterling silver fork she liked to slip in the trash.

The other change that came over the household after my father retired was more subtle. I began to notice when I visited that the mood between my parents had lightened, become less dangerous. Household alliances had shifted. As my father became more frustrated with my sister, he and my mother, after decades of raging, sniping, and discontent, seemed to have called a truce, or even better. They began, hesitatingly at first and then more openly, to be kind to one another, conciliatory, tender even.

Of course, my perspective on their relationship was relatively recent. They'd been married twelve years by the time I was born. I knew there had to have been a time when they'd been more than kind to one another. I'd seen traces of it in old pictures and, years later, cleaning out my parents' things, I came across letters tucked far back in drawers, first one from him to her and then ten years after that, one from her to him, in a wallet my father had saved from his Navy days. Fifty, sixty years old and tearing at the folds, these letters were proof of something so piercingly sweet and private I never made it past the first line of either one. Until this late phase of their marriage, though, I'd never actually witnessed it.

Now, instead of their tired old arguments and their absolute and arbitrary disagreement on all subjects, they began to defer to one another. These kindnesses were so small at first, these domestic negotiations so internal, they sounded trivial when I described them to anyone else, even to my brother who knew the territory as no one else did. But small as these changes were, the weather had changed.

I theorized what the cause might be—my first thought was that maybe all my father's churchgoing was finally taking effect. Or maybe it was because they were drinking less, or maybe now that he was home, my father had finally come to appreciate the difficulty of my mother's life. Or perhaps, I thought, they just had time to talk now. What didn't even occur to me was that my mother was dying.

It must have been obvious to them. Maybe they, diehard if frustrated romantics, saw this as their last chance to make up. Whatever it was, whenever I visited I could sense that the potential for psychological violence, which had formerly hung so low in the air, had lifted. It felt safe to be there, fun even. They told affectionate stories about one another, called each other rascal. They took picnics to the park, packing up hard-boiled eggs and sardines and filling their blue china teapot with ice and martinis, their old ruse for sneaking booze where it wasn't allowed. When my brother visited, they gave us a joint birthday dinner with a happy birthday paper tablecloth, cake, and candles. They sang. Our birthdays are a month apart; the whimsy of an extra celebration wasn't their style. When I thanked them, my father, who'd handled the food and logistics, said, "It was Mom's idea."

A small thing in another family, maybe, but in mine it was a watershed moment, not because my father had given my mother credit but because he'd agreed to her plan in the first place.

This sense that my parents had joined forces at last came clear one afternoon in the little third-floor apartment I'd moved to after breaking up with Jeff. My parents had come for Sunday dinner, and when my phone rang, there wasn't much privacy. They sat at my kitchen table eating cheese and crackers as I spoke with my therapist, who'd called to reschedule my Monday appointment. After I hung up, my mother asked who'd called.

I could have obfuscated. I knew it was a bombshell. But the proximity of my shrink, just a phone call away, made me feel brave, like experimenting with truth and disclosure, a radical, reckless thing in my family, the equilibrium of which had been built on carefully preserved secrets and held-back opinions.

"My shrink," I said, pouring us all another drink.

My parents looked stricken, embarrassed, as if I'd confessed to something so intimate they didn't feel entitled even to express disapproval. Pressing my advantage—my father for once was speechless—I said she'd helped me. I even told them her name was Barbara, knowing my mother's childlike affection for anyone who shared her name. Then a strange thing happened. My father turned to my mother and coaxingly said, as if to a child, "Maybe you'd like to go see Margy's therapist. Maybe I could take you there." My mother averted her eyes and shook her head a little. "We'll see," she said. It was her standard reply. It meant "hell no."

It never came up again, with me at least, but the exchange had been a glimpse into their private world. My usually secretive mother was confiding something in my father that worried him enough that he'd set aside one of his most deeply held prejudices to try to get her help. Somehow it all seemed to have to do with my sister.

It reminded me of another glimpse I'd gotten a couple of years earlier. My father had been walking me to my car after dinner at their house and took the occasion to tell me my mother wasn't eating. "She feels guilty," he said. "About Barb." He whispered the word *guilty* as if it were an obscenity, though we were standing in the driveway and no one else was around. "She's acting the way she did after Tom was born," he continued in his urgent whisper, as if I knew all about that, as if it were something he and I had discussed at length.

I mulled it over for years afterward. It didn't make sense. The two events—my brother's birth and my sister's illness—were completely unrelated. Whatever guilt my mother felt about my sister couldn't possibly have anything to do with her postpartum depression forty years before that.

Unless it did, I thought, but only later. Maybe my mother's paralyzing anxiety wasn't a psychological response to life events but a physical, biochemical condition that predated them. Maybe it was aggravated by stress and manifested as guilt but maybe it had been there all along. Maybe, I thought, my mother's moods were as uncontrollable as my sister's voices. Maybe they came from the same source.

Chapter Fourteen

In the summer of 1996 my parents declined an invitation to come to my place to celebrate my mother's seventy-fifth birthday. I'd moved again the preceding fall, this time into a house with Fritz, and my parents, especially my mother, loved to visit. That winter, on the nights they'd come for dinner, my mother sometimes drifted away from the table mid-meal, and when I went looking for her, I'd find her lying on the couch or in one of the beds. Once I tracked her down and found her under the covers in the guest room. "It's so peaceful here," she said, as if in explanation.

We played many Parcheesi games at the dining room table that winter, my mother with her magnifying glass at the ready to examine her dice. My father by this time had risen to new heights of solicitousness and had even taken over her grooming. He filed her fingernails, washed and combed her hair. At last his mania for control had flowed into a place where it was needed. Now that they weren't fighting, they were fun to be around, like two charming, highly imaginative, white-haired children. My father would zip up my mother's winter coat for her in our hallway before they went out into the cold, buckle her seat belt for her, scold us for refilling her wineglass too quickly. Fritz couldn't understand why I'd ever complained they were difficult, and it was too complicated to explain, especially since they were on their best behavior around him. So when my mother didn't want to come to our air-conditioned house for dinner at the height of a July heat wave, it was a sign that something was wrong.

When we arrived at their house, the problem became clear. My mother had a black eye. She had a black eye because she'd fallen. She'd fallen because she was too weak to stand. She was too weak to stand because she'd stopped eating.

By August she couldn't get out of bed. My father redoubled his cooking efforts to coax her appetite back to life but it was no use. He brought her food on trays—artful, appetizing little portions arranged in the center of child-sized plates—which she refused to touch. Ice cream, sherbet, Jell-O, toast, clear chicken broth he made from scratch, even tiny martinis. She'd take a bite or a sip and turn away. Food, the very thing he most believed in as remedy and recreation, had finally failed him.

I started to bring her food, thinking maybe it was another twist in their complicated relationship and that her resistance was only to him. One day I brought ripe pears, her favorite, which she accepted with a weak smile and then stashed on the far side of the bed. My father discovered them days later when they began to rot. I brought cans of Ensure she politely declined, which my father took to swigging to keep up his own strength. He began sleeping on the couch to be near her bed in the den. He stopped going to the gym, stopped going to church, stopped going out altogether except to shop for food she wouldn't eat.

Of course she wouldn't go to a doctor. When I offered to look for someone to make a house call, my father demurred. Then early one September morning I awoke to a ringing phone. It was my father calling to say he was at his wit's end. His words, those. I remember them exactly because this admission of helplessness—an admission that his wit in fact had an end—was unprecedented. He wanted to know if I would try to find someone to come to the house after all.

The doctor came that afternoon and several times more and, after checking everything he could without admitting my mother to the hospital, determined she was basically healthy except for the fact that she was starving herself to death.

Barb, already remote, all but disappeared during these weeks, particularly when the nurses and social workers began to show up, though sometimes on her way to the kitchen as she passed the darkened room where our mother lay, she leaned in and called out, "Hello!" Finally one Friday morning in October, my mother didn't wake up. My father called an ambulance, then me, and we met in the emergency room. My brother arrived the next day, and there we all stayed for eight more days until my mother died.

During those eight days, we took turns going to the house with food for Barb. Usually by the time we got there she'd already made lunch and washed the dishes. When I told her Mom was in the hospital, she didn't react. She hardly seemed to notice she'd been left alone.

After my mother died—it was a Saturday morning—my father and brother and I went back to the house. My father immediately set about making a casserole. Tom and I went out to rake leaves. When Barb came down for lunch I told her what had happened. "Aha," she said, and went back upstairs to consult with her voices.

I took the next week off work, spending much of it at the house, cleaning out my mother's closet and dresser. She didn't own much, had never been interested in things, and now they seemed more an irrelevancy than ever, something that had nothing to do with her, to be cleared away as soon as possible. And I needed to do it. The thought of my father going through her things was too sad.

He was happy to stay downstairs and cook while I sorted everything into three piles: one to throw away, one to give to charity, and one to keep. I filled garbage bag after garbage bag with clothes, and as I worked, Barb stood silently in the doorway, now and then handling a garment or some object, saying, "Can I have this?" I was a little surprised she was interested. I started to call out to her—Do you want this sweater? These towels? Padded coat hangers? She'd come in to feel the fabric and consider and then disappear into her room again. That was all, but it was something new, a real exchange on her terms—clothes and fabric had always been something she understood.

Two weeks later, we held a memorial service for my mother at the church and a reception afterward at my house. My sister did not attend either one.

Chapter Fifteen

Barb never did seem to acknowledge or react to our mother's death, and between her disconnectedness and my father stoicism, their household routine resumed almost immediately. My mother's presence, especially in her later years, had been essential to the psychology of the family but not to its practical operation. That was my father's domain, and he reinstated his routines with a vengeance after she was gone.

He seemed to be trying to make up for lost time. Every morning he got up early to swim, in the summer rising at 5:00 a.m. to ride his bicycle to the community center for twenty-five laps in the outdoor pool. Then he hurried home to cook breakfast for himself and Barb—bacon, eggs, toast, oatmeal, fried potatoes, coffee, sometimes also pancakes or cookies for my ninety-pound sister. They were both wiry by now, with not an ounce of fat between them. My father, who had lost all his extra weight caring for my mother, stayed that way by doing what he called his chores—shopping, laundry, tending his flower garden, shoveling snow, raking leaves, trimming bushes—working through his arthritis.

My sister spent her days talking. Her high-pitched fervor had quieted over the years, her language was no longer obscene, and she seemed to feel a little less preyed upon by accusatory invisible third parties. But still she mumbled furtively from early morning on, still seeming to report on what the invisible others were telling her, still starting sentences with the words "Now they're telling me . . . " and only stopping for the huge, hearty midday dinner my father cooked while drinking his daily martini. This he served in the kitchen promptly at noon. She ate it standing up, at the other end of the house at the desk in the hall, and then disappeared upstairs, leaving him alone for the rest of the day. In the late afternoon he took her tea and a snack upstairs on a tray. Usually by 5:00 p.m. she had retired to her narrow bed in her dark room.

With my mother gone and only Barb to look after, my father's enormous free-floating energy demanded a new focus. He began to make new friends and deepen his relationships with old ones and, particularly, with his neighbors.

The neighbors had always been able to find my father in the yard, working in his garden in the summer or shoveling snow in the winter, and often stopped to chat. Now they began to include him in their lives, inviting him for dinner, for their children's birthday parties, for outings to baseball games, basketball games, concerts. They sneaked over early in the morning to shovel his snow, plow his drive, rototill his garden, deposit his newspaper on the porch so he wouldn't have to negotiate the treacherous front steps. One day he casually let it drop that some young neighbors had taken him to a Cubs game and afterward dancing at a club across from Wrigley Field, a club I remembered going to in the eighties, with Jeff. We'd seen punk bands there. My father was reinventing himself again—in his ninth decade.

Alice Roosevelt famously said of her father Teddy that he wanted to be the corpse at every funeral and the bride at every wedding. My father was a little like that. Certainly, he wanted to get as much out of the rest of his life as he could, and for him, that meant being the center of attention. His hunger for an audience, though, made an odd pairing with my sister, whose attention was elsewhere, focused on voices even more insistent than his. My father, who loved to talk, tell stories, crack jokes, recite poetry, argue, philosophize, lecture, and expound, was living with someone who did not and could not listen to any of it, someone with whom he could not have a real conversation. He didn't complain—to the contrary, he insisted that my sister was good company—but the more she withdrew, the more social he became. Or perhaps it was the other way around. Whichever it was, my father didn't expect more from Barb at that point. His plan was just to keep her there as long as he could and to live as long as possible.

Chapter Sixteen

After my mother died, my father wrote his will. The delay—my father was seventy-nine—may have resulted partly from denial, but it also came from my parents' disagreement over what the will should say. My mother thought anything they had should be divided equally among their three children. My father wanted to arrange for it all to go to Barb. Now that my mother was gone, he could do as he liked.

After months of back-and-forth with his lawyer, my father presented my brother and me each a copy of the will in May 1997, my brother's mailed to him with a terse note, mine handed to me as I left his house after yet another Sunday dinner. Earlier in the day, we'd gone to Rosehill Cemetery to put lilacs on my mother's grave. Afterward we returned to his house to eat. I noted in my journal that night that he'd served baked ham, fruit salad with kiwi, vegetable casserole, homemade cornbread, and for dessert a yellow cake with chocolate frosting he'd made himself. He may have been planning for death, but he was still very much alive.

As he handed me the bulging envelope with my childhood name written across it, he gave a grim Nixonian salute, a gesture eerily like the famously aborted wave the ex-president made minutes after his resignation. And I suppose that's how this felt to my father, like a resignation. The acknowledgment of his own death felt disgraceful to him, like giving up. To die meant to forfeit the game, and he hadn't planned to do that. Not that we'd discussed it much; it made him too mad. Over the years, whenever someone asked what would happen to my sister after he and my mother were gone, my father would bristle and say he planned to outlive her. That usually ended the conversation. Now, at seventy-nine, he was admitting he might not.

When I got home I threw the envelope onto a pile on my desk. I planned to ignore it for a long time. The next night, after a couple of glasses of wine, I sat down and read the whole thing. My father had placed everything in trust for my sister. I was her trustee.

It wasn't a surprise, exactly, and I couldn't argue with the logic. My brother and I could support ourselves. She could not. Nor could she manage anything left to her. I lived nearby, it all made sense. But it felt like an intentional slight and I spent the next few days in mild shock, feeling like a backpack full of rocks had been strapped to my shoulders, trying to get used to the weight, which would either pull me over or, if carried just right, straighten my spine. Either way, it made it very difficult to move.

It's only a will, I told myself. I don't have to do it. When the time came, I could blow it off, leave it to my brother. There was even a clause for that, *If the trustee should be unable to execute her duties,* something like that. I could become conveniently *unable,* go AWOL, leave town, leave the country. Let Tom figure it out.

I knew I wouldn't, though. It was a burden but one I'd always expected. And more than that, it was my long-delayed opportunity to change things, a chance that felt like unfinished business, the culmination of the twenty-year argument I'd had with my father. Cagey as always, he'd bet on my stubbornness. "You think you're so smart," he seemed to be saying. "Fine, you handle it then."

My father and I never discussed the will, nor did we discuss my sister's future or either of our intentions for it. We'd given that up twenty years earlier when the subject only led to argument. Heated as those discussions had been, though, they were theoretical. Now what we would have been talking about was too real, too close, and too scary. Neither of us wanted to think about his death, and I didn't want to hear some burdensome request I'd later feel obligated to fulfill. Specifically and selfishly, I didn't want him to pressure me to promise to move Barb into my house to care for her as my parents had, though it was my constant worry that I should, that this was exactly what he and the world at large expected of me. Once, years before, he'd said in his most sentimental way, after we'd both had too much to drink at lunch, that he imagined one of us—referring to my brother and me but clearly meaning me—would build "a little house for Barb out back" as the neighbors had done for their elderly father years before. At the time, all I could think of was Mr. Jones and how when little girls took him May baskets, he'd stand in the doorway and slyly part the folds of his bathrobe like theater curtains to display his musty crotch. That my father now romanticized that arrangement made me furious.

I'd wondered then, back in the eighties, if my father really expected Jeff and me, who did not even have a pet, to build a little house "out back" for Barb behind our Chicago bungalow, against code on our thirty-foot wide lot, attached perhaps as a one-room shack to our one-car garage. Now, ten years later, Fritz and I had a little more space, but still, zoning aside, I wasn't ready.

Chapter Seventeen

A few days later, my friend Kim dropped by my office and asked what was new. I told her about the will. She proclaimed me Job. No, I said, no. But I appreciated the sympathy. In fact, I wanted it. I showed her a Karl Marx quotation, the exact wording of which I had looked up in Bartlett's the day before. The book was still lying open on my desk. "From each according to his abilities, to each according to his needs." For me, that summed it up. "What about your needs?" she said.

Then she asked me what I would do when my father died. People had been asking me that for twenty years. My therapist used to bring it up, but we never discussed it. I always found a way to turn the conversation back to men. I told Kim I couldn't think about it.

She pressed. "Will you keep her in that house and have someone come in and stay?" I said I didn't want to talk about it. But there was an idea.

I sat at my desk for a while, unable to work, and finally walked down to personnel and asked for information on health insurance, hoping whatever they gave me would include mental health but not wanting to ask. Sure enough, there it was. If I went back into therapy, I could get a half-price deal up to a thousand dollars' worth. It wasn't much, but it would get me a few months, more or less, depending on what my old therapist was charging these days. I wondered if I could just discuss my sister's options or if it would be like my meeting with the university psychiatrist twenty-five years earlier and we'd have to talk about me first. I didn't feel like doing that.

I almost completely avoided talking about Barb in those days, especially at work. I was working at a collectibles company, and part of my job was to write sappy sayings about the joys of family life, about mothers, daughters, sisters. By then I'd written hundreds of sugary platitudes about how great it was to have a sister. A sister, I said, was a lifelong friend. A confidante, a champion, a soul mate, someone to go shopping and grow old with, someone to tell your secrets to, someone whose shoulder you could cry on. A sister's love was a gift from above.

Writing these kitschy tributes to ideal sisterhood was more than a sham but one I was uniquely qualified for. It put me in touch with my fantasy of what I was missing, a fantasy unmarred by the petty rivalries and downright meanness I'd observed in more normal sister relationships. My copy had the overheated corniness of the outsider who wants in, a cloying earnest poignancy no one else's could touch.

The irony felt so stark I came to assume it had some instructive, karmic purpose. Although my life was not orderly in those days, I believed in order, or I tried to. I believed in karma and that we had many lives in which to learn and make mistakes and then correct them. I believed we were here to teach each other and that my sister was here to teach me a thing or two. Although mainly so far, she'd been teaching my father. I considered it likely that in a few years— who knew when—they would meet up somewhere in the afterlife in some vaporous form and throw the electromagnetic counterpart of arms around each other's shoulders and say, "Well done, comrade! Now there was an interesting course of study." Casting off their mortal coils, they would no longer be father and daughter, super-conscientious Depression-era, stalwart, stoic, gin-loving Wasp and fragile schizophrenic. They would be two glowing nimbuses of infinitely wise energy.

Sometimes I really believed that.

Here are some of the sayings I wrote in those days. Sisters Share a Special Warmth, Sisters Share Triumphs and Tears, Sisters are Blossoms in the Garden of Life, Sisters Wish on the Same Star, Sisters Share Each Other's Dreams, Sisters Know Each Other by Heart.

It was only a matter of time, I reasoned, before someone turned to me, the writer of all this treacle, and asked, "Do you have a sister? Is this how you feel about her?" I'd even rehearsed an answer.

But no one ever asked. I knew the exact family composition and birth order of everyone I worked with, which ones had sisters and which had daughters, who was on the outs with whom, and all of everyone's names. They freely discussed themselves, their families, husbands, wives, children, siblings. I was the only one who never volunteered information about my family. What would I have said?

A few days after I read the will, I began keeping a journal about Barb. Suddenly it felt like I needed to keep track.

May 26, 1997

Memorial Day. I'm happy to have no plans. Tonight Fritz and I will grill hamburgers. I'll make garlic green beans and we'll eat the dill potato salad I made yesterday. We'll see a movie. Maybe tomorrow we'll touch up the rust on my VW, take a bike ride. I'll plant some geraniums in pots for the front porch.

What will my sister do today? She will lie curled in bed and talk to herself. She will hover in a doorway and mutter. She will scuttle around the house, up and down the stairs to goad my father about meals. "When do we eat?" she will call from the upstairs landing. "Hold your horses, kid," he'll growl back. He calls her Kid or The Kid. She is fifty-two. I will not visit them today. I visited last weekend. Thinking about visiting them makes me feel like taking a nap. Next weekend we'll celebrate my father's eightieth birthday.

Chapter Eighteen

Three weeks later, in June 1997, my father flew to Raleigh, North Carolina, to visit Tom and Anna for Father's Day weekend. Except for the eight nights we spent with my mother in the hospital, it would be the first time in many years that Barb would be alone. I promised my father I'd check on her while he was gone. He worried she'd leave the stove on and burn down the house. I worried she'd be lonely.

He left early Friday morning and planned to return Sunday night, so on Saturday around noon I drove to the house, rang the doorbell, waited on the porch and, when I didn't get an answer, let myself into the kitchen. Barb had been alone one full day and night, and I didn't know what to expect. I called her name and at first she didn't answer and then she did and while she made her way downstairs, I snooped around. Stove, sink, bathroom—all seemed okay. When she appeared in the kitchen she seemed happy to see me, though not especially anxious for company. I asked if she wanted me to make lunch—my father had left enough food for a month— but she said no thanks, she'd already cooked herself bacon and eggs.

Alarmed, I looked again for damage but, except for a faint aroma of bacon, noticed no signs of cooking. The kitchen was clean, the dishes had been put away, and the house had not burned down.

It appeared that, after one day on her own, my sister had already expanded a little. Again the radical thought—what if she just stayed there? By herself? Maybe I could hire someone to help, do the shopping. I could use whatever money there was, that mysterious amount which I did not know and of which we would never speak, to support the house. I couldn't do everything, but I wouldn't have to. I would visit, supervise, introduce stimulating advancements, even treatment of some kind. I wrote these ideas down in my journal that night, so radical and unusual they seemed to me then, as if they would disappear in a mist if I didn't record them immediately.

But Barb's ability to cook and clean up for herself wasn't the only difference I noticed that day. She wanted to talk, with me.

Sometimes when I visited we had short conversations when we were alone, say, when my father was distracted by a particularly tricky kitchen procedure, but not often because we were seldom alone. But now we were, and she wanted to talk about current events. She asked me what was happening in the news. I told her about Timothy McVeigh's trial for the Oklahoma City bombings. She said she found that hard to believe and, looking thoughtful, added, "There's a lot of bombing going on." I couldn't disagree, especially when she proceeded to list places around the world where this was true. Then she said, "Where do you suppose that puts us on the sex and violence spectrum?"

She waited for me to stop laughing, regarding me probingly as if to gauge my thoughts on the subject, then answered her own question. "About in the middle, I think."

I told Fritz about it when I got home. He said he didn't know you could have conversations like that with her. I'd known, but I'd forgotten. It had been a long time since Barb and I had talked.

Over the next weeks I read and reread the will and began to make lists of expenses:

Real estate taxes

Utilities—gas, electricity, water, phone

Upkeep on the house: plumbing, etc.

Housekeeping

Lawn care

Snow removal

Food

Clothing, incidentals

Caretaking—residential or biweekly visits to include services such as grocery shopping, laundry, light cleaning, cooking

Medicine?

Below these calculations I wrote:

"Fantasy: I get my old therapist to come visit Barb. The cost is all covered. She turns me onto all kinds of possibilities for care, benefits, compassionate and creative mental health people. What a concept. Too bad this can't happen during Dad's lifetime."

Chapter Nineteen

As soon as my father returned from Raleigh he began planning a second trip, this time to visit his brother in Florida. When I called him on a Tuesday, two days before he was to leave, I caught him packing. He was getting it out of the way, he said. He planned to spend Wednesday "laying in casseroles" for Barb.

That Friday, Fritz and I adopted a sixty-four-pound puppy from Sav-a-Pet animal shelter. It was something I'd wanted to do for a long time and the decision felt momentous. Max was rowdy, handsome, sweet, high-spirited, destructive, alarmingly intelligent, boundlessly energetic, strong, and huge, a Rottweiler-shepherd mix in need of serious training. We loved him right away.

On Sunday morning we took him back to the shelter for their early morning obedience class and afterward to meet Barb. It was already beastly hot by the time we left the class—Max had not excelled, we were all frustrated—and by the time we reached the house, an hour's drive away, the temperature was in the nineties and still climbing.

Max was droopy and tired from the heat, the stress of so many new experiences, the failed training session, and the hour-long car ride, and so were we. But I had a plan and would not be deterred: pet therapy. I would introduce Max to Barb while my father was gone, and he would cheer her up, puncture her isolation, get through to her on levels no longer accessible to mere humans. We'd only had him two days, but my idea was that Max would change her life by working the same magic on her that he already had on me.

Instead, when we got there she was hot and cranky, and when I brought Max in she was afraid and annoyed, angry that the house was so hot, angry with me for bringing the dog. He was too big, too wild, too strange, too scary. After galloping around the house and briefly sniffing Barb—she stood rigid and terrified and scowling—Max sized up the situation correctly: she wanted nothing to do with him. So he left her alone and collapsed in a heap on the cool kitchen floor while Barb retreated upstairs to rant loudly about prison, suicide, rape, masturbation, bombing, gas attacks. Always in the third person—the others were telling her, she said.

I offered to bring the fan upstairs, but she said no, suggested opening the windows, which my father had left open for her and which she'd closed, but she said no. I considered doing it anyway but didn't want to make her any angrier than she already was and knew she'd only close them again. The temperature continued to rise. The hottest room in the house was her upstairs bedroom, the one in which she was hiding from my dog. The visit was a disaster. She didn't want us there, and she wanted nothing to do with Max, but I felt guilty leaving. The heat was dangerous. I wondered if I should send Fritz and Max home and stay overnight whether she liked it or not, but finally I didn't and we ended up leaving her there in her own private hell, while we went home to our air-conditioned house.

It wasn't even one in the afternoon when we got home, but immediately we fell into bed, the three of us, exhausted from the heat, the drive, the failed obedience training, the failed visit and, for my part, the failed effort to avoid thinking about my sister in that hot house, her future, and her dark thoughts, which spilled directly into mine.

My fantasy that Max would effect a miracle cure had proved ridiculous. I drifted into an uneasy sleep, hoping to dream my recurring dream that Barb was well.

Chapter Twenty

A month later, in August 1997, my father called to say he'd decided to add my name to my sister's guardianship document if that was all right with me. The idea was that when he died, I would become her legal guardian. I said yes—that was the extent of our discussion—and he proceeded to set up a court date.

The day it happened, September 26, 1997, I didn't make a journal entry. Maybe I didn't fully recognize how this event would change my life. Or maybe I did, and didn't want to think about it. The only reason I know the date now is that it is stamped on the document. Every time I handle it, I remember the day.

My father has planned our route to the Circuit Court of Cook County in minute detail. I am to pick him up at his house on Friday morning at exactly nine o'clock. He's ferocious about my not being late. I surprise him by being early. I don't remember seeing Barb or if we tell her where we're going. I doubt it. Probably we assume she won't understand or maybe we think she'd be upset, though now it seems like it might have made her feel more secure. Maybe we don't even consider it.

My father gets in my car and tells me exactly where to drive, when to stop, when to start, where to turn, where to park. I park at the L stop at the end of Cumberland. We are to take public transportation from here. I am relieved. I don't think I can bear having him as a passenger all the way into the city. Start, stop, slow down. Pay attention! He is a control freak though I am the better driver.

We board the train; he uses his senior citizen CTA pass. We get transfers, board a second train. My eighty-year-old father who's never actually lived in Chicago negotiates the CTA better than I do. We get there in good time, way too early in fact, which is his maddening lifelong habit, though now it serves a purpose. He needs extra time to drag around his arthritic leg. He refuses to use a cane.

I slow my gait as I walk beside him. We make our way slowly to the courthouse, find our way slowly to our courtroom, and sit for a long time on the hard benches waiting for my sister's name to be called. Finally we hear it—Shallal—it doesn't sound like her, it doesn't sound like us, but it is. Now it's our turn. We rise, walk up the center aisle, my father limping slightly, and stand before the judge.

She reads the request out loud and begins to ask my father questions. He tells her about my sister. He describes her behavior, her history, her life with him. The judge sets down the paper, leans forward, and looks at him over her reading glasses. "Do you mean to tell me you've never gotten her any medical help?" she says.

He says that is correct, then explains why and ends with something about not trusting shrinks.

"How long has this been going on?"

He tells her it's been going on for over twenty years. He is direct, defiant in his honesty, makes no effort to varnish the facts or justify his behavior. She sighs, sits up straight, rattles her paper, exhales audibly. Does a little pantomime. Shock. Disapproval. Exasperation.

Finally she leans toward him again and says, "There are drugs that can help in these cases, you know." Then to soften it, she adds, "They're better these days than they used to be."

It is a kindness, that she says this. She's showing him she understands there were no obvious choices, understands that it hasn't been easy. One look at him tells her that. Standing before her, he must look small, exhausted, old—all his charm and pep and humor and ferocity bleached out of him by the institutional setting, the effort of the trip, the pain in his leg, the story he's had to tell yet again. She sees all this and is trying to help.

Then she turns to me. Pauses for effect. "Someday this will be in your hands," she says. "I hope you'll do things differently."

We lock eyes. I smile slightly and nod just once, wanting to make this connection but not wanting to insult my father or arouse his wrath, set him off. Even here in court, I imagine him throwing a fit. "I plan to," I say. I almost whisper it—or do I only imagine having said it, expecting him to fly into a rage? But whether I say it out loud or only to myself, I mean it. I do plan to do things differently, and this makes it official.

Later, when my father is handed the document, titled Plenary Guardian of Estate of a Disabled Person, naming us both as Barbara's legal guardians, he is taken aback. It names us jointly—his plan was for me to be named his successor. He actually winces. Paranoia flashes across his face—this is not what he intended—and I can read his mind: what if I try to seize the power?

But he doesn't need to worry. I've learned to pick my battles, and I'm in no hurry to take over. Almost ten years later, as my father is dying, I retrieve this same piece of paper from his safe deposit box, drive to Kinko's, and make dozens of copies. After he dies, I keep a sheaf of these around, at my house, at her house, and pass them out every chance I get. It is my permission slip—I'm in charge now—and my passport in the land of public aid. Every time I look at it, I remember my promise to the judge.

Chapter Twenty-one

In those days I read a lot of books about mental illness. I didn't think of it as research, just my default topic of interest if nothing else at the bookstore caught my eye. I see from a list I kept that in a one-month period in the spring of 1998, I read *An Unquiet Mind*, Kay Jamison's book about manic depression; *Wasted*, a memoir by Marya Hornbacher, a precocious bulimic girl who, in one lost weekend of binging and puking, clogs the family plumbing and then breaks the pipes with the volume of her vomit; and *My Sister's Keeper* by Margaret Moorman, an art writer with a much-older schizophrenic sister.

The obvious parallels to my own life in this last book particularly captured my interest—later I'd even write for the same art magazine—and I found myself hungrier for Moorman's story than I was for her sister's. The book wasn't meant to be her personal history, but the details she did mention—giving up a baby for adoption, a suicide attempt, both while she was in high school—were tantalizing. I wanted to know the whole story up through the present, if only to compare it to mine, maybe to see how my life would turn out, though by any conventional timeline it already had.

Even though I was squarely in middle age and living a busy life—love, work, travel, friends, family, house, newspaper column, dog—I had the feeling sometimes that things had not yet begun, that I was standing outside my own life. When my gay friends talked about how it felt to be closeted, I thought I had an inkling of what they meant, though they looked at me funny when I said so. They thought I was trying too hard to be sympathetic, but what I meant was that I knew how it felt to be hidden. Often I felt like there was some other, more authentic me locked away somewhere waiting to come out, waiting for the full weight of responsibility for my sister to settle upon me so that I could begin my real life.

One day my father told me excitedly about an article Tom had sent him from *The New York Times Magazine* about Dr. Torrey's brain bank. Tom, whose job as news director at the National Institute of Environmental Health Sciences kept him informed of the latest medical research, often sent my father and me clippings about mental illness. This one was about Torrey collecting and studying the brains of dead schizophrenics to find the origin of the disease. My father was less excited about the brain bank than he was about the rest of the article, which caught the reader up on Torrey's history. It repeated the basic positions of his book—dismissal of most psychiatrists' handling of schizophrenia, scorn for insight-based therapy, which he believed was actually harmful, and strong criticism of the profession for making parents feel guilty about their children's disease.

My father felt vindicated, thrilled that someone was trashing psychiatry, even if it was a psychiatrist doing the trashing. He kept the article on the kitchen table in a position of honor next to his running grocery list. I was happy for him, but what was strange was that this was 1998, thirteen years after someone had given my parents Torrey's book saying the same things. My father acted like this information was entirely new. Again, I wondered: Had he not read the book or even the two-page summary? Had he read it but then forgotten? How could he have forgotten something so crucial and potentially helpful? Or had he been in such denial and despair then that he couldn't accept hopeful news if it wasn't the hopeful news he wanted? Again, the old anger washed over me as I wondered if my sister could have been helped if only my parents had been willing to take someone's advice, if only they'd been a little more open, a little less secretive.

Around that time, I drove to Iowa to cover an exhibition at the Des Moines Art Center and detoured through Iowa City to visit my cousin Kate. In our meandering conversation that night, we covered a lot of old family pain, including our grandmother's suicide. I wanted to know more. I'd been named for her, and the fact that she'd killed herself so close to my fifth birthday had always felt to me like a bad omen. For starters, I wanted to know for sure if her death—by drowning—even was suicide. No one had flat out told me. When I asked Kate how she knew, she said her mother had just told her, had sat her and her brothers down and said she was sad because their grandmother had killed herself.

Betty was a professional psychologist; of course she'd known how to handle it. But the contrast to my experience—which amounted to my mother going to bed and crying for a year for no explained reason—was stark even from a distance of almost forty years. In my family, such directness was unthinkable. Instead, an unmentionable sorrow had hung over our house, as dark and turgid as an August storm cloud before it bursts. Years later, my mother's sorrow still seeped out at odd moments. Once, upon hearing news of some troubled neighbor boy's suicide, she burst into tears and fled the room. When I followed her to the kitchen, she sobbed that her mother had never owned a house.

Sometimes my family's secrets were so well kept that even those who once knew them forgot what they knew, and maybe that was the real point. We kept secrets not to hide things from the world but to hide them from ourselves. In the hospital as my mother lay dying, a nurse checking for hereditary conditions had asked my father how his wife's mother died, and without hesitation he said Parkinson's disease. He wasn't lying. He'd just decided to forget.

Chapter Twenty-two

March 19, 1998

I called my father tonight. He told me that Barb had worn a new white sweater and said that when he asked her where she'd gotten it she'd said I gave it to her. I don't remember, but as I told him, I have given her so many sweaters over the years, it may be one I gave her long ago. He was pleased she'd saved it and worn it though he disapproves of my giving her so many clothes. She has too many, he says.

I ventured to suggest that I think it's okay she hoards clothes because it's nice to have something new when you feel like wearing something special. He said he thought her "acquisitiveness" was a symptom of her "ailment." He remembered when she was in Iraq and wrote to him (he said him, not us) and asked that he send her quantities of luxuries . . . 24 bottles of Prell shampoo, 14 bottles of Chanel No. 5, and 18 bottles of Charlie perfume. I knew it was true because he never could have come up with Charlie perfume on his own. He said he'd sent a few of each but made a point that he had not filled the excessive order. He has told this story many times. He is always outraged by the acquisitiveness of it.

I said I thought she'd shown signs of hoarding before. I was thinking of her drawers full of mohair sweaters, her ironed hair ribbons and later, after she got sick, her stashes of Scotch tape, toilet paper, note pads.

He sounded disappointed when he said, "I thought she was always kind of spartan—like me." I said I didn't think so but didn't elaborate. I didn't want to hurt his feelings or start a fight. But then he changed the subject. I've noticed he does this often these days. He doesn't want to discuss my sister or any family problems for long. He clings to safe positions and corny attitudes, gets mad if anyone tries to budge him, like his sudden fury when I told the social workers who came to try to talk my mother into going to the hospital that she'd suffered from depression. He blew up, lashed out at me like I'd told some outrageous lie. It was awful to be attacked for telling the truth.

The trouble with mental illness is that you start to look at every flaw and quirk in the family of the sick person and wonder if that's what made them sick. It isn't fair, especially with this disease. Lots of families keep secrets and never have to contend with this. It is important to keep all this separate but very difficult to do so.

···◆···

March 22, 1998

[My friend] Deb was here for the weekend. We sat up until two a.m. talking after dinner. I told her about Margaret Moorman's book and her saying that it's common for siblings of mentally ill people to put their lives on hold, that they can't begin anything because they have to anticipate what may happen with the sibling. Or maybe this is just my problem and has nothing to do with my sister.

Deb said she always remembered my sister as a princess, as a terribly glamorous person. Beautiful but not only beautiful, she said.

Reading Moorman's book makes me wonder again about joining a support group to discuss care options. When I think about it, though, I feel exhausted, as if it's one more thing on a long to-do list.

Once again, I think hopefully about the possibility of hiring a social worker to check up on her so that she could continue to live independently in that house. Although the house would need some major work.

There are these issues:
his health
her health
money
longevity—hers
longevity—his
her potential after—might she change
her willingness to cooperate with treatment options
treatment options

Moorman writes about her dread of having a child, says she was afraid of having a sick child, like her sister, and was afraid she'd react to motherhood with intense depression, like her mother. These were two of her big life fears. Mine too. Unlike me, though, she risked it.

· · · ◆ · · ·

April 7, 1998

I had lunch with my father yesterday. I wonder if he is not doing well. The lunch was fine but not as fancy as usual. Usually he puts on a feast. He was grouchier than usual too. I know he's in pain from arthritis, not that he talks about it. I don't know what to do about him sometimes. I'm glad he's so independent. I am relieved both for him and for myself. But sometimes I wonder what I should do for him. Talk him into moving out? He will be eighty-one in two months. If it weren't for my sister, I would bring it up at least, but what would happen to her if he moved? Would he take her along? Move her into a two-bedroom condo? That would be hard enough. But if not that, then huge choices would have to be made and huge agreements come to.

He can't take care of that house forever; we both know it. He mentioned that his next-door neighbor sold her house and moved to a condo, "like an old lady should," he said, and he continues to be interested in how much he can sell his house for. The neighborhood is full of teardowns. Mrs. V sold hers for a good price, and today they're knocking it down. By this time next year, there will be a new house there with a three-car garage, five thousand square feet of living space, and a Jacuzzi in every bathroom. My father's house will soon be surrounded by these enormous places. Already it looks like the groundskeeper's cottage on someone else's estate. The day he sells it, they'll knock it down.

Though I'm sure when the time comes he'll be happy to have the money. It's just the transition that worries me. The other thing that worries me about his moving, other than Barb, which is the big thing, is the yard. He loves his yard and the seasonal work Raking, mowing, gardening, even shoveling. If that's all gone, what will he do?

So I went to lunch yesterday at my father's. My sister drifts around like a little ghost and drifts away if you pay too much attention to her. She admired my sunglasses and my skirt. She called it a maxi, a perfectly accurate fashion word in the mid-seventies when she last followed these things. I told her the weather was warm and invited her to go for a ride in my car as I often do. "Oh no," is what she always says to this suggestion, as if I've invited her to do something outrageous, like jump out of a plane. I said, "Come on, we can put the top down." And she said, "You have a convertible?" This is a ritual we have. She always acts surprised, though I've had this car for eight years. I can't decide if it's elaborate politeness on her part and she's humoring me, pretending to be interested because she thinks that's what I want to hear, or if it's a game.

Every summer I offer to take her for a ride, and every time I do she acts surprised and pleased, then flatly refuses when I press. I no longer expect her to accept my offer, but I still wish she would, since riding around with the top down is one of my great simple pleasures and I would love to share it with her. She always says no.

This exchange represents the basic sadness of her condition. There is no way to share pleasure with her. It slides off her, she refuses to absorb it or is unable to. I wonder sometimes if this is her illness or something else, something dark I recognize in our family psychology, some perverse minimalism or worse—it is my father who loves to cook and yet has a barely equipped kitchen, and sometimes it is me too.

····◆····

December 15, 1998

I haven't written here lately, been absorbed in my own life. Sometimes I can do that, forget about all this. Christmas is coming, so I try to think of ways to delight my sister. Always I give her underwear, piles of it. I have a rule—I only buy her what I'd buy for myself. No better, no worse. When I shop for myself, I buy for her. My father doesn't understand it—why does she need so many "pants" as he calls them. What does she do with them?

It depresses me to think of the level of detail of my sister's life that my father monitors. Almost every time I talk to him, he complains about how fast she eats. This has been going on for decades. It drives him crazy. And it must drive her crazy that he constantly harangues her about it, except that she already is crazy. Ha.

Long passages of time can go by without any real change on this front. One notable thing did happen, though. On her birthday, in October, I had lunch at my father's. He made beautiful food, and we gave Barb presents. I bought her a bunch of clothes, more underwear. Fritz gave me a jar of white pepper to give her. Tom sent a notebook and a pen. She opened the pen and, to test it, wrote on the back of the packaging, "M&B love you." A few days later, I received a thank-you letter written clearly and cogently on a note card my father had provided and posted. It said, "Dear Margy, thanks a lot for the loveable shirts. I'm glad you had fun. It's raining now. Dad had fun, too. Say hello to Fritz. See you soon. Love, Barby. P.S. Thank Fritz for the nice pepper!"

It was the first letter I'd gotten from her in twenty-five years, and what was strange was that it wasn't that strange. No doubt my father had coached her but still. I wrote her a chatty letter back. I told her I was reading *Winesburg, Ohio*, and offered to lend it to her, but that was the end of the exchange.

Time passes, and I don't see or talk to her. My father comes here more than I go there. We invite him for meals. It relieves him of his responsibilities and gives him a treat, I think. Plus we like to cook for him. He was here for Thanksgiving along with a bunch of our friends—a big fun party with flowing champagne and a turkey and home-baked pies and our rambunctious dog. And she was home alone. Of course she's always invited. But she won't come. Sometimes I imagine she'll just show up one day.

I think all the time about what will happen, who will die first, who will take care of whom. Will there be enough money to make it possible to get her help, to not just maintain, perpetuate this exhausting, passive catering situation? I feel guilty and morbid for thinking about money and death all the time, but someone has to. I am the one who has to plan it. I dread becoming the caregiver and feel ashamed of that dread. Last night my friend Diane was here describing the bone-tiring task of caring for her two normal kids and trying to work at the same time. It sounded awful, but they'll grow up.

It occurs to me apropos nothing that my dog probably weighs more than my sister does.

· · · ◆ · · ·

June 1, 1999

Last week my father was diagnosed with prostate cancer. This week he has a bone scan to see if it has spread. Tom has been calling and researching treatment options and sending research available to him at work and that he's found on the Internet. This helps because though I can do the research, I can't discuss things like castration and impotence and incontinence with my father. Of course this raises the question of what happens next with my sister. What will happen when and if he is too sick to care for her but still well enough to raise major resistance to doing things differently? This is my real fear—having to take care of him and her while putting up with his assaults on me the whole time. Sometimes I am so angry in anticipation of this I can't think.

Saturday is my father's eighty-second birthday. He told us not to buy him anything except for a woman's headband he saw at Walgreen's that he plans to use as a new hatband on his straw hat. We'll give him food.

· · · ◆ · · ·

June 29, 1999

Since I last wrote here, my father had his consultation after the bone scan. I went along to take notes and lend moral support. At first he didn't want me to go, seemed to think I would take over or that the doctor would ignore him and talk only to me. So I tried to keep quiet and avoid eye contact with the doctor. What we learned is that although his PSA [Prostate Specific Antigen] levels are incredibly high, the cancer has not spread to the bones or the lymph glands, the two places this kind of cancer is likely to go. So this was extremely good news. The doctor recommended hormone therapy, which will reduce the PSA and keep the cancer from spreading. Life will go on as usual. No surgery and no side effects even, except for loss of sexual function, the doctor says, looking at me. I realize he thinks I am my father's wife. This is disturbing in more ways than one. I must look really old.

I pretend not to be, but I am uncomfortable sitting next to my father while the doctor holds up an enormous set of larger-than-life brightly colored pink plastic testicles attached to a giant dangly penis. The whole contraption is hinged at the middle and he holds it open, viewable in cross section, while he talks about erectile dysfunction. Ejaculation. Hormonal castration. Afterward, we're both so relieved it's over and that he's not really sick and that there are no signs he will become sick, we go out to lunch to celebrate. I have to get back to work, so we go to a nearby coffee shop and split a tuna salad sandwich and an order of fries. As we're leaving, my father wraps the extra fries in a napkin to take home to Barb.

When the doctor mentioned the possibility of cancer in the bones, he said it would mean there was a "two to two-and-a-half year projection." "Projection of what?" my father yelled, instantly furious, daring the doctor to say it. He couldn't believe the doctor was talking about his life span that way. *His* life span.

But thinking that way, thinking of two years out, is a whole different way to look at the world for me. In two years, I would assume full responsibility for my sister. And it may still happen then, or sooner. Then there will be decisions to make. What if I moved her near here, I wonder, sell the house they're in and buy one closer to us, have someone visit her, prescribe something or just radically alter her diet?

There was a story in the newspaper while we were in Boston about some doctors at the University of Florida trying to eliminate autism and schizophrenia in children by cutting carbohydrates and dairy products from their diets. Wouldn't that be easy to retest, prove even? I want more info on this. Too easy to be true I suppose, but what a concept.

If I were in charge I could experiment with these things.

· · · ◆ · · ·

July 24, 1999

All summer it has been hot, hotter than usual even, in the nineties often and edging toward one hundred and over. I wonder about my sister. Does she suffer?

There was an article in today's *New York Times* about measuring happiness. They now say it's mostly a function of brain chemistry, genetics, but that certain conditions affect it, like having friends, and that money doesn't, in the long run.

So what of my sister? Is she happy?

Chapter Twenty-three

By mid-2000 my father had finally begun to make concessions to age. With Fritz's help, he'd managed to fly to Raleigh for Anna's funeral—she'd died of ovarian cancer in September, and I'd gone early to be with my brother—but that was the last time my father flew. He still drove, mowed his own grass, clipped his own hedges, swam laps most mornings, descended the steep basement stairs to do laundry several times a week, and cooked daily meals, but he was slowing down. He fell off his bike and didn't get back on, resigned his post as head usher at his church because it bothered his leg. Sometimes he figured out imaginative ways to adapt—carting his groceries from the garage to the back door in a wheelbarrow, cooking whole meals in the microwave—but the one thing he couldn't imagine, and refused to even discuss, was what would happen when he could no longer do everything himself. So he just kept going, postponing the inevitable moment when he, and Barb, would be forced to accept assistance.

That's when he began to talk, though derisively, about moving to a place without stairs or a lawn. He grudgingly toured a new condominium development near his church. Of course he hated it, or said he did, but the real problem wasn't adjusting to a move. I suspected he'd grow to like elevators, dishwashers, common rooms with computers and chatty neighbors who'd teach him how to use one. He'd refused my old Mac on the grounds that his fingers were too arthritic for typing, but I knew Fritz's teenaged daughter Steph could get him hooked on email in fifteen minutes.

The problem was my sister. She wouldn't leave the house. He couldn't go without her. And even if he could convince her to move, how could they, and Barb's voices, coexist in a condo after all those years in a two-story house?

I started to wonder if it was already too late, if it might just be easier for my father to stay where he was and hire help, except that he wouldn't do that either. Which brought me back to the question that kept me awake at night. If he became unable to take care of himself and Barb but still insisted on being in charge, what then?

I tried to think of where I could turn for advice, or whose advice I'd be willing to hear, and remembered John Spear, an artist I'd written about a few years earlier. John had a day job as a social worker doing street interventions with homeless schizophrenics, sometimes taking them art supplies and getting them to draw and paint.

When I'd visited his studio, the tour culminated in the kitchen, where he showed me gorgeous, shocking paintings by his schizophrenic clients, which he kept stashed in a portfolio on top of his refrigerator. That he valued this stuff was a very good sign. If anyone would have a perspective I could tolerate, I thought, it was John. I called him up and asked about our options.

"Group homes," he said, naming several in the area with good reputations. "Get her doctor to put her on waiting lists."

I explained.

"Hmmm," he said. "Any psychiatric paper trail at all?"

"No," I said.

"Not good," he said. Group homes had requirements, a certain number of hospital admissions usually, or at least a current diagnosis.

Next he recommended enrolling her in a day program. "She needs to be observed," he said. "To see what kind of care she'll need."

I explained about her not leaving the house.

"Daily home visits from a nurse or a social worker then," he said, advising we start now, while my father was still around, so the presence of someone new didn't destabilize her when he died. This time I didn't bother to interrupt to explain how impossible even that was.

He must have sensed my despair.

"Ask her what she wants," he said. "Ask her how she wants to live when your father's gone. Does she want to live independently? Or would she prefer a place where people could help her? Get her to start making simple choices," he said. "And do it now, so it won't be such a shock when the time comes."

I said we'd assumed she couldn't make decisions, that she didn't have opinions. Or that if she did, they'd be too outlandish to accommodate.

"Don't be so sure," he said. "She may not be as helpless as you think."

Chapter Twenty-four

As my father got weaker, he began by necessity to agree to conveniences he'd formerly resisted. He hung a tag in his car that entitled him to easy access parking, hired landscapers and a cleaning lady. He saw each of these concessions as a small defeat, a giving in to luxury, but the fact that he made them at all was promising. By giving up a little independence he could keep most of it longer, and I hoped he might eventually accept help with Barb too. But any discussion of her future meant a discussion of his death, and he wasn't ready for that. Somehow we had to plan on the sly.

Early in the spring of 2004 I called my friend Deb, who was by now CEO of a mental health center in central Massachusetts, and asked her for references in Illinois. Two days later she called back with a list of names. It took a few days to connect with the right person, but finally I reached Amy Smith, a social worker with Thresholds, a private agency in Chicago, who said she handled cases like Barb's and would be happy to make a house call to meet her.

Bull's eye. Except, no.

I explained why she couldn't actually meet Barb. Could she come to my house though, to meet my brother and me? "Sure," she said. "Any time." So we made a tentative plan, and when Tom next came to Chicago, in August, the three of us met at my house.

Tom and I told Amy my sister's history. She nodded, unsurprised.

She had other clients who lived with their parents, she said, though they were all on meds. She told us she worked with a family nearby—elderly parents, schizophrenic son in his forties. "Sometimes he's violent," she said. Sometimes he needed to be removed, though they always brought him home afterward.

Removed? We wanted to know how they "removed" a violent forty-year-old man when we couldn't get Barb to take a walk around the block. Her reply was matter of fact. "We usually call the police."

Tom and I blanched. This was exactly what we dreaded. But Amy's matter-of-factness was exactly what we needed to hear. She was telling war stories, maybe to scare us into doing something before it was too late.

We talked for hours. She told us about housing options. Like John, she recommended getting Barb on waiting lists for group homes, thought there might be some way around the usual requirements. I was stalling, saving my big question for the end, like the patient who tells the doctor about the pain only after he's climbed off the examining table and put his clothes back on. Finally, as Amy was getting ready to leave, I said, "What about keeping her there?" I said it so softly I had to repeat the question so she could hear me. I was afraid to speak up, afraid she'd just say no.

Instead, she shrugged. "Maybe," she said, but there was no way she could make that judgment without seeing Barb. She'd just have to see, when the time came, how well Barb could do on her own.

Amy didn't sound particularly hopeful, but she didn't sound unhopeful either. As John had been, she was practical and unemotional, the opposite of us. Then she handed us each a business card and told us to call her when something changed.

That night, Tom and I had dinner with our father. Neither of us mentioned Amy.

Describing the progress of this research makes it seem almost orderly, but at the time it didn't feel that way. It felt desperate and disconnected, not to mention stealthy. Trying to reconstruct these various interviews later, and place them in time, I dug through a pile of old notebooks. There I found notes from my conversations with Amy and Deb and John mixed haphazardly with everything else in my life from those days, buried almost.

I can date these conversations by the notebooks they're recorded in, by the other dated entries that surround them, but the notes on Barb are mostly undated and scrawled between grocery lists, notes from art exhibits I was writing about, a list of questions I planned to submit to a veterinarian about the cat I'd just adopted, ideas for a travel story on Toronto, recipes, notes from a trip to Ireland, quotes from an artist who'd built a puppet theater on the back of a bicycle.

I'd buried my research on Barb under the conveniently messy details of my daily life in a way that now seems intentional. To dedicate one orderly chronological notebook to this subject wouldn't have been so hard, but it would have required me to acknowledge that it was necessary, that this ongoing project merited focus. I couldn't do that, couldn't admit that I needed to. In contrast, I look at the orderly file I began for Max the week we adopted him. Even on my best days I'm not very organized, but somehow I'd managed to keep every receipt from every veterinary visit filed chronologically, along with Max's weight recorded in an orderly dated column, readable at a glance. Would it have been so difficult to keep a similar file for research on my sister? Apparently.

Chapter Twenty-five

My father made it through Christmas of 2005 on sheer will and almost no food, but by the first week of January 2006 he was in constant pain and so weak he could barely walk. Then early one morning a few days into the new year, my phone rang. It was Richard, my father's neighbor, who'd called to say he'd found my father on the couch, groaning and cursing in pain, refusing to go to the ER.

It took me almost an hour to get there, and I still had to argue, then wrangle, him, furious, into the car. Finally, after getting him to the hospital and medicated into unconsciousness, I called to thank Richard. "There's something you should know," he said. Someone had summoned him from the kitchen window. He'd seen an urgent wave as he walked past the house and, assuming it was my father, let himself in. But when he got inside, my father was in the next room, immobilized by pain.

The person at the window had to have been Barb.

It was a Boo Radley moment. Barb had stepped out of the shadows to do what needed to be done and then disappeared again, nowhere in sight by the time Richard got inside the house. It was another hint that my sister, who had withdrawn so much from our lives and from her own, was still in there somewhere.

But I didn't have time to think about that. My father was in the hospital and Barb was alone. Someone needed to manage things, and the job fell to me, flowing into the vacuum where my paying job had been. A few months earlier I'd quit, with the uncertain plan of remaking my life—writing, teaching, living on savings—but work wasn't exactly pouring in, at least not the paying kind.

So every morning I drove to the hospital to check on my father who, after a lifetime of loathing doctors, was enjoying the benefits of modern medicine. I'd arrive to find him sitting up in bed, bright-eyed and rosy-faced, telling stories to a laughing circle of nurses and orderlies. Then I'd drive to the house to check on my sister.

Word hadn't gotten around yet that my father was in the hospital so the friends and neighbors who for months had been dropping off daily provisions to spare him the effort of cooking continued to do so. The scale of their ongoing effort to keep him and Barb well supplied was now apparent. No matter what time of day I arrived, I'd find plates, bags, and covered dishes piled at the back door. Whole roast chickens, platters of homemade cabbage rolls, salads, pastries, soups, desserts, loaves of fresh bread, an entire pork roast, once even a loaf of challah bread—whence came that in my father's very Gentile suburb? I never knew. My father's circle of friends was wide and the donations were all anonymous.

Once I got inside, staggering under a tower of food, my sister seemed perfectly fine. She'd usually decline my offer to make her lunch—she'd already eaten and washed the dishes by the time I got there—and instead offered to make me tea.

It was a small courtesy, hardly worthy of mention in another family. But for my sister to extend this ordinary gesture of welcome was extraordinary. And strange. For some reason, when my father was gone she was different and not only different but better, more social, more self-sufficient, more considerate even. And the improvement wasn't gradual, it was instant. I looked forward to our visits, would sit down at the kitchen table and make a point of not putting the tea on, waiting for her to offer and then offer to add milk, just the way

I like it.

When I brought my father home from the hospital almost a week later—they released him too weak to walk in the middle of an icy snowstorm at that suicidally gray four o'clock hour that is a typical January afternoon in Chicago—he was frail and wobbly but determined to recover. Soon his energy—and temper—returned. For a while I went every day, and I noticed that as my father recovered, my sister retreated. Our daily tea ritual evaporated, and the spark of connection we'd had while my father was gone disappeared as well. So I forgot about Barb for a while as my father's demands grew greater, louder, more dramatic.

Everything was harder now, but he was determined to continue living as he had. For the next few months, with regular visits from a physical therapist, some help from Tom and me and a lot from the neighbors, but mostly through sheer will, he returned to his life. He kept his doctor's appointments, resumed driving, shopping, cooking, and waiting on Barb, and for a few months even resumed his routine of visiting us on Sunday afternoons, making his way slowly up the front walk, leaning on his cane with one hand while carrying a freshly cut bouquet from his garden in the other.

In April, he was diagnosed with bladder cancer. Still, he kept going. Never mind the trips to the emergency room and the program of daily radiation treatments that left him exhausted, or the increasing trickle of grifters who started to show up in his life, mistakenly thinking they could rip him off just because he was old and weak, mistakenly thinking his mind was in any way impaired. Never mind the fall in his garden, when his axe stuck in green wood, a fall from which he couldn't get up, occasioned by his disbelief that sheer will could not win out over old age. Never mind the demoralizing and miserable medical procedures, the daily bus rides to the hospital, the long waits and endless corridors, the ongoing struggle to communicate with an ever-expanding assortment of doctors, nurses, and technicians, and the fury their incomprehensible jargon and often hard-to-understand accents roused in him. He just kept going—in pain and refusing help for it—as he clung to his increasingly tenuous independence.

He was angrier and angrier. He shouted at anyone within earshot, and those most often within earshot were my sister and me. The long-standing contentiousness of our relationship became more so as I lost my temper with him when he was least able to control his own. He was frustrated and angry—angry that he was old, angry that he was in pain, angry that he was ill, angry that he had so much unfinished business, angry that I'd bought him the wrong brand of toilet paper, and most of all, angry that he had to do the one thing he swore he'd never do: depend on other people.

As always, just when I was on the verge of murdering him, he'd do something sweet. Once, after dropping him off in the ambulance lane at the emergency room—with relief I'd handed him, shouting and swearing, over to a beefy orderly with a wheelchair and sped off to park my car—I returned to find him subdued and medicated, sitting in a plastic chair across from a nurse twice his size. As I approached out of sight, I could hear him apologizing, telling her contritely, "I'm sorry. I know. My daughter tells me I should try to be nicer." I was amazed. It was no surprise that I'd arrived at the end of yet another confrontation. The surprise was that he was citing me in his apology.

His greatest strength was his biggest problem. The stubbornness that kept him going was the same thing that made it impossible for him to listen to any plan for his own care, let alone for Barb's, who by now hardly engaged with him at all. She simply withdrew, taking care of her own needs and ignoring his.

By the end of summer, he began to decline more precipitously. When my brother had visited in May and taken him for an eye exam so he could renew his driver's license, my father not only passed, he was licensed to drive without glasses. By fall, though, he'd stopped driving for good.

By mid-October, I was checking on him every day. So were

his neighbors who kept bringing food, which by now he mostly only pretended to eat but which spared him the effort of trying to cook for Barb. He kept losing weight. The pain was worse. He could hardly move. He disdained the idea of help as much as ever, but finally he was too weak to resist and agreed to talk to Joyce Garb, the social worker I'd put him in touch with years earlier and whose services he'd firmly rebuffed ever since. I now had two agenda items I wanted her to press on him: caregivers and pain relief, which he'd adamantly and completely refused after a bad experience with Ibuprofen. I hadn't been able to talk him into it, but maybe she could.

Joyce warned me up front she was worried about finding a caregiver. It wasn't my father, she said, brightening the way women usually did at the thought of him. It was my sister who was the problem. She seemed hostile; she might scare them away.

Here was a whole new problem to worry about, one I hadn't even thought of, which seemed so strange as to be almost funny. With me, Barb was courteous, compliant, almost meek, while my father was constantly raging. With Joyce, though, my father was courtly. To her, my sister was the scary one. It was a long-standing dynamic—my hyper-social father charmed the neighbors and saved his venom for us; my hermetic sister did the opposite. Together they were a tag team, two sides of the same face, who seemed to trade off personality traits to either draw in or repel outsiders as it suited them.

Joyce showed up at my father's house the next Friday with Rosa, a nurse and manager from the agency that supplied caregivers. I got there as soon as I could, expecting the worst, but by the time I arrived, one look told me we'd been rescued. With some combination of authority, kindness, and tact, Joyce and Rosa had gotten my father to agree not only to caregivers but also to drugs.

Rosa immediately called in a prescription for a morphine patch. Joyce arranged for the caregiver, Karen, to come twice a week, four hours each on Tuesdays and Fridays. I had argued for daily visits, but my father resisted, demanding the minimum. Even at two days a week, he fretted there wouldn't be enough for a caregiver to do and, mostly, at the idea of a stranger taking over his kitchen. But four hours was the minimum, so the plan was set for Karen to arrive at nine the following Friday morning and stay until one. She would shop, clean, prepare meals for the rest of the week, do the laundry, take out the garbage, and otherwise do what I'd been doing. It would be eight hours a week during which my father wouldn't have to lift a finger, eight hours a week I didn't have to worry that if he fell there would be no one there to help him.

On Friday mornings, I taught in the city. My class ended at noon, and on Karen's first Friday, I rushed madly back through sleet and traffic to arrive at the house before she left, dreading what I'd find when I got there. What about my father's profane outbursts? What about my sister's resistance to strangers? What about the creaky plumbing?

But when I arrived, I found Karen and my sister companionably discussing the next week's lunches—the very fact that Barb was downstairs at that time of day rather than barricaded in her room was remarkable—while my father sat at the kitchen table composing a grocery list. All the lights were on, the house was clean, and in four hours a subtle shift had taken place. This easygoing woman from Belize would now control my father's kitchen and even his grocery money for two mornings a week for the next few weeks, and though he shouted instructions and fretted about whether she was spying on his finances, he accepted her presence, respected her work, and did his best to get along with her.

Chapter Twenty-six

On Thanksgiving morning, Fritz and I got up early to roast a turkey breast. We'd baked pecan and pumpkin pies the night before. We made stuffing, sweet potatoes, mashed potatoes, cranberry sauce, gravy, and green beans and took half of everything to my father's house in time for lunch, the only possible time of day to catch him with anything remotely like an appetite. My father watched with mounting horror as we unloaded the food, and it was only when we got it all out of the bags and onto the table that we realized this scaled-down version of Thanksgiving dinner, which had looked so modest in our kitchen, appeared grossly excessive in his.

At my father's request, Fritz mixed them both martinis, and while they sipped their drinks, I made a plate for Barb, then went out to look for a pharmacy. The morphine patch wasn't working. I'd gotten them to up the dose by phone the night before but hadn't thought to fill it then, and now it was Thanksgiving and every pharmacy was closed. He'd have to wait another day—not good news.

While I was gone, Fritz made my father a plate of food with baby-sized portions—a tiny piece of turkey, one green bean, a dollop of cranberry sauce, a teaspoonful of mashed potatoes, another of stuffing—and sat with him while he tried to eat. When I got back, all the little portions were still sitting on the plate. Finally, my father gave up and made his way slowly, slowly back to bed. He wasn't feeling well, he said, and fell asleep almost immediately. We stayed awhile as he slept, then cleaned up, put away the food for Barb, and went home. Around eight, the phone rang. It was his friend Amy, who lived across the street, calling to say an ambulance was leaving my father's house. He'd called 911.

Chapter Twenty-seven

Except for a few paper turkeys stapled to bulletin boards, Thanksgiving in the emergency room is like any other day there, which is to say it is like no day anywhere else in the world. All natural signs of time are absent. There are no windows from which to watch as evening becomes midnight; all light is artificial and searingly bright twenty-four hours a day. Movement is either urgent or excruciatingly slow. The boredom of waiting is punctuated by cops rushing by, hands on guns, by moans escaping from triage rooms. Doctors, who all appear to be children in costume, shamble about avoiding eye contact and staring at clipboards.

As usual, my father made a miraculous recovery, and by the time we'd tracked him down, he was sitting up and making conversation with a pretty intern, looking years younger than he had hours before. We'd just been through this, a month earlier, on my birthday; he'd recovered so quickly that night, they released him. This time, though, they wouldn't let him leave.

The next week was a blur of tests, room changes, meetings with doctors, therapists, social workers. By the time I got to the hospital every afternoon, there were new test results to comprehend, new experts to track down, new problems to worry about.

Barb, in the meantime, seemed fine on her own, better than she had just days before on Thanksgiving when she'd flitted in and out of the kitchen for food and otherwise disappeared. Every day when

I stopped by on my way home from the hospital, she asked about Hawkins, as she called my father. When was Hawkins coming home? I kept telling her it would be another few days, though I hoped it wouldn't be that soon. He was too weak.

They started talking about releasing him, though to where was the question. I kept trying to buy more time, agreeing to tests just to keep him in the hospital a little longer, where he was safe and comfortable with a twenty-four-hour staff and serious pain medication on demand. Where he wanted to stay.

My father, who'd rejected all these services at home, welcomed them now. He wanted to stay. "Just give me a few more days," he'd tell anyone who asked, "until I feel up to leaving." I think he planned to return to his old life. He wanted to get his strength back so he could resume grocery shopping at Jerry's, his favorite bargain produce market.

The doctors shook their heads. There was nothing more they could do, they said. According to policy, he had to leave. They recommended moving him to what they euphemistically called a rehab center. He knew what that meant and said he didn't want it. I asked him what he did want and he said if he couldn't stay in the hospital, then he wanted to go home. So I told the doctors I was moving him home but they didn't like that idea, so I said, "Well, you tell him, then." I'd spent the past year translating increasingly grim prognoses to him. I wasn't going to be the bearer of the worst news yet.

His doctor agreed to meet with him the next morning, and by the time I got there, full of dread, as usual, it was all settled. My father had negotiated a deal. If he showed them he could walk, he could go home. Maybe the doctor had meant to prove to my father that he was being unreasonable, but if so, he'd underestimated him. In one last act of sheer stubborn, death-defying will and with the aid of a walker, my father got out of his hospital bed and made it down the hall to the window and back. He was going home.

The next day, at the doctor's suggestion, I met with a social worker from Rainbow Hospice, but I did so guiltily. My father hated the idea, hated the word. For him hospice equaled death. I explained to her things might go more smoothly if nobody used the H-word around my father. I tried to explain that he was the kind of guy who cared about words, even now. Especially now. I tried to explain how some words made him mad and that hospice was at the top of his list. Did she suppose they could call it . . . palliative care? Okay, she said gamely, but she must have been thinking what an absurd request it was in light of what she knew lay ahead. In a few days, an army of helpers would descend on the house with other things on their minds than my father's feelings about language. But I couldn't yet think about that, couldn't imagine what was about to happen or how all this personnel would interact with him, let alone with Barb.

We got a reprieve over the weekend, but I was informed that on Monday my father would have to leave the hospital. I called Rosa and asked her to send back caregivers—this time for round-the-clock shifts. I made arrangements to get a hospital bed delivered.

On Monday morning, I went to the house to prepare for my father's arrival. I moved furniture, climbed into the hospital bed and tried out the remote control on all the movable parts, while Barb stood silently and watched. Around noon, Rosa showed up with Leticia. I'd been hoping for Karen, since my father and sister already knew and liked her, but she wasn't available until later in the week. Here, instead, was this tiny Filipina grandmother who didn't speak much English. She immediately took over the house. She'd been a math teacher, she said, and I could see it. She treated me like a slightly below-average student in need of extra credit. The first thing she did was make a shopping list and send me out to fill it. By the time I got back, my father was home, delivered by ambulance, and Leticia was in charge.

I remembered Joyce's warning about caregivers and my sister. Suddenly three people were living in the house where only two had been, and soon I would move in. How would my sister adjust?

A few days later, I heard her in the kitchen with Leticia. Barb, sounding slightly annoyed but uncharacteristically focused, was saying, "Are you telling me what to do?" The question was rhetorical. By then Leticia was telling everyone what to do. The strange thing was that my sister seemed to rise to the occasion, accepting some of Leticia's bossing around and shrugging off the rest with admirable self-confidence. Barb was around more too. Partly it was the food— Leticia was cooking robust meals three times a day, not for my father whose appetite hadn't improved much, but for my sister and herself— but it was also Leticia's energy that attracted her. As Karen had briefly before, Leticia was restoring order to the house.

There's something strangely comforting about hospice, despite its inevitable ending. It has an unplugged do-it-yourself feeling of gliding in on your own power, akin to what I imagine it must feel like to fly one of those planes without motors that surfs the airstreams like a kite and eventually drifts earthward. We—it was a fluctuating *we*— lived there together for a little over two weeks. First it was just Leticia and my father and Barb with a continuous stream of visitors including nurses, assistant nurses, social workers, chaplains, friends, neighbors, members of my father's church, Fritz, Max, and me. Then Karen arrived and I moved in—one caregiver didn't seem to be enough, and someone had to stand on the front porch at midnight to wait for the morphine delivery. Then a different Karen came, this one with cats tattooed up and down her arms—then my brother arrived from North Carolina and moved into an upstairs bedroom, then Karen left and Leticia came back, then Fritz brought Max and stayed.

For the first time in many years, the house was full, brimming with people from all over the world. Leticia was Filipina, Karen was from Belize, the chaplain was Cuban, the nurse who sang gospel songs in a booming voice that filled the house and brought everyone in it to tears, was African. My father was dying, but the house was more alive than it had been in years, decades.

My sister managed this strangely lively interlude with surprising—to me—equanimity. She didn't seem at all bothered by having extra people around, though clearly she was agitated by the medical part. She was talking more, responding more to her voices than she had in some time—in the same shifting balance I'd noticed earlier when my father was in the hospital, the quieter he became, the more she talked, not to us now but to herself, intensely and incomprehensibly mixing real medical words with her private made-up ones.

One afternoon felt especially strange. It was dark, yet another gray December day, and just the four of us were there, my father, Barb, Leticia, and me. Leticia was trying to explain something to me in her heavily accented English, which was fine for talking about food, but which, when she had complex observations to make about my father's condition, I couldn't understand. At these times, she communicated by looking up words in the dictionary and pointing to them, following me around the house, the huge book cradled in one arm while she stabbed her finger at the words on the page—*comatose, hallucination*—and then stared at me to make sure I understood. I nodded and turned back to my father.

I was trying to understand what he was whispering. He wanted me to pay attention. This man who had demanded to be listened to, this man of speeches and lectures and recitations, whose voice was now inaudible, wanted me to understand him, but I couldn't. Just then, my sister passed us on her way to the kitchen, mumbling made-up medical jargon in conversation with her voices. There we were in the house of Babel. In what seemed like a parody of my family's lifelong obsession with language, I couldn't understand a word anyone was saying.

· · · ◆ · · ·

My father died on a Tuesday night, after fifteen days at home. We'd been expecting it for days, the nurse had predicted it for days, surprised that he continued to live when his body seemed to have long ago used itself up, stubborn and economical to the last. My brother and I sat on either side of him. His breaths came slower and slower, farther and farther apart until finally they stopped, as simply as that. Fritz arrived minutes later, with Max. We three sat with him for a while and then I went upstairs to get my sister.

She was in bed, awake. I told her Dad had died. She nodded. I asked if she wanted to come down to say goodbye. She said, "I thought you said he died." I explained what I'd meant. "Okay then," she said, and followed me down the stairs and into the room where his body lay on the bed. Tom and Fritz sat on either side. Barb and I went to the bed. I stood behind her. She stood looking at him for a minute, and then I asked her if she wanted to touch him. She leaned over and pressed her hand into his arm, withdrew it, and said, "Amen." Then she went back upstairs.

Chapter Twenty-eight

I remember the winter light I woke to the next morning and, weak as it was, how unbearably bright it seemed. Hospice had been a comfortable dark cocoon, and I wanted to stay there, quiet and cared for. But I couldn't—too much had to be done.

Tom and I began to call the list of people who needed to know. We met with my father's minister, met with the funeral home director, wrote the obituary, planned a memorial service, wrote checks, cleaned the house, moved the hospital furniture out, called more people. People called us. Neighbors came with food. We picked music, shopped for food, bought champagne, planned a reception. We wrote eulogies. Our cousins flew in, Deb flew in. And four days later—two days before Christmas—we gave a memorial service at my father's church and afterward a reception at the house.

I was determined to do it. I wanted to clear the house of the process and smell of death, bring it back to life. I didn't want anyone's last memories of my father to be the smell of disinfectant and the blue flicker of his broken TV. I wanted to dig out the beautiful dishes that had been in storage for years, the stuff my parents had so nonchalantly used in better times, the old candlesticks, the frayed damask linen tablecloths, the Limoges serving platters, the family silver. After fifteen days of mixing morphine-laced Hawaiian punch cocktails for my father, I wanted candlelight and wine and good food for his last party.

My brother, who was staying in the house with my sister after I'd moved back home, pointed out that the plumbing was ancient and bad despite an emergency visit from a plumber the day before my father died. He pointed out that it might simply burst from use if we had people in, and not only that but that the floorboards were rotten and liable to open up and drop everyone into the basement. He was right, of course, especially about the iffy plumbing. It was a risk. But we had to do it. It was the only way my sister could attend.

The memorial service was joyous and beautiful, with music, poetry, storytelling, and much humor. The group that adjourned to the house afterward was more festive than mournful. Tom and I stayed at the church until everyone was gone—Fritz and Steph went back early to welcome guests—and by the time I got to the house, the reception was in full swing. It was a long time before I made my way from the kitchen to the front of the house, a long time before I noticed the cluster of people standing in the front hall, surrounding a small person dressed in black. Here were my friends and there among them, pale and drawn but present, was my sister.

In the avalanche of organizational details leading up to this moment, I had completely forgotten about her. But there she was, holding a glass of wine and a small plate of food, talking to Kim.

Chapter Twenty-nine

The next week was an anxious blur. Tom stayed with us on Christmas Eve, then returned to the house Christmas afternoon to stay with Barb for three more days. After that, he'd leave for Raleigh. What, I wondered, would I do then?

For two months I'd relied on the support of Covenant Methodist Senior Services, the agency that had provided my father's caregivers. Now I missed them. I missed Rosa's efficiency and compassion. I missed the security of being ordered around by Leticia. I missed the first Karen's easy humor and the second Karen's casseroles and cat tattoos. I wanted their attentions to continue indefinitely. I wanted them to take care of me now. I wanted not to be left alone.

A few days earlier, I'd called Laura Solomon, CMSS's director, to explain our situation and throw myself on her mercy. What should I do now? I'd asked. Had she ever heard of such a case? Couldn't they just keep coming? Couldn't they take care of Barb now? I felt like I was in a dark tunnel, and probably my questions were not that clearly formed. Please help, was more like it.

Laura and I talked for at least an hour. Or mostly I talked, she listened. Mental health care was not her agency's usual domain, she said, but she'd try to figure something out and agreed to meet with Tom and me on his last full day in Chicago. She came to us, first to the house to meet Barb, then to a neighborhood restaurant where we talked for another two hours. Tom and I each told her our version of family history, and when we were done, Laura said she'd see what she could do. The next day, I drove my brother to the airport.

I was alone with Barb.

Our parents on their wedding day, October 24, 1942, in Winnetka, Illinois
My father, fresh from Officer Candidate Training School, was then an ensign in the
U.S. Navy. For the next two years he and my mother traveled around the coastal
U.S. to Naval training and duty stations, from Staten Island, New York to Beacon
Hill in Boston to Norfolk, Virginia to Key West, Florida to San Pedro, California to
Tacoma, Washington, until my father was shipped out to the Philipines to serve
on a minesweeper.

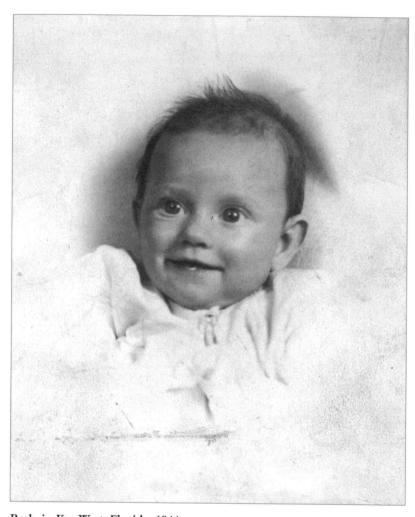

Barb, in Key West, Florida, 1944
As soon as my mother could travel after Barb was born, she packed up her
newborn and joined my father in Key West, where he was stationed.

Barb with Dad, in his garden, June 1954

FROM ALL OF US | TO ALL OF YOU

a Merry Christmas
AND A HAPPY NEW YEAR

Barb, Tom, and me, Christmas 1954

JAN 1955

Barb and me, January 1955

1955

Barb, Mom, Tom, and me, 1955

Hawkins family, 1956

Me and Barb, with Timmy the stuffed bear, Christmas 1959

Barb, 1960

Barb, with her beloved Underwood typewriter, 1961

Mr. and Mrs. Karim Shallal on their wedding day, December 31, 1966

Jain Yurtis, Barb, and Sharon Kazmar at Barb's wedding reception
Barb and Sharon met in high school, where they worked together on the staff
of the creative writing magazine. Barb later became friends with Jain at the
University of Illinois.

Barb and Max on the couch, 2008

Barb and me, Thanksgiving 2009
Fritz took the picture, Barb planned the menu—smoked salmon,
saltine crackers, olives and champagne.

Barb and Max on the back porch, summer, 2008

PART II
2007

January

The simple facts of our situation as they stood on January 1, 2007, were not so simple. The stubborn independence that had served my father so well in life had left Barb, and to some extent me, stranded after his death. Barb was very ill—anyone could see that if they saw her at all, but almost no one did. She was nearly invisible. Even those of us who knew she was there didn't know much about her—not my father's friends and neighbors, not his church, not the medical establishment, not the extended family, not even Tom and I.

What I did know was this: Barb lived alone. She had no contact with the outside world. She was completely dependent on me, and I lived twenty miles away. In perfect weather and light traffic the drive from my house to hers took thirty minutes—in the winter, much longer. I couldn't spend all my time taking care of her. I had to make a living. And, although I felt guilty about it, I did not want to spend all my time taking care of her. She couldn't stay at the house alone without help, but she wouldn't leave. She didn't appear to be interested in communicating with anyone. She wouldn't answer the door when the doorbell rang or the phone when it rang. She hadn't made a phone call in thirty years. She'd never even seen a computer. She had no systematic way of getting food, though if people dropped it off, she'd eat and even cook a little, and she had no awareness of money. She couldn't have cared less that real estate taxes were due and that monthly bills were piling up on the porch, let alone that gutters needed to be cleaned, furnaces checked, and lawns mowed.

The obvious solution was to "put her someplace," as everyone called it when I started to wonder out loud about what I was going to do. Even that wasn't simple, though. Unless she agreed to go, that option required force as well as legal action, and that was only possible if she qualified as a risk to herself or anyone else, which she didn't seem to be—although we didn't even know that for sure because she'd never lived alone. And even if we all agreed that putting her someplace was the best thing to do, she had no psychiatric history, no doctor, no connection with any system that could suggest a place based on any knowledge of her needs or abilities. All the advice we'd been given was to get her on a waiting list, but even if we could get the requirement for a psychiatric paper trail waived, we'd been told that when an opening came up we'd have to be prepared to move her immediately. Since that meant she would have to agree to leave at a moment's notice or be taken by force, we hadn't done it.

On top of all this, I had another, more basic problem with putting her someplace. It didn't seem fair. It seemed like an abuse of power, a preemptive strike, a last resort solution to a problem we hadn't even begun to try to solve more civilly. It seemed like cheating, skipping from step A: denial and inaction, to step Z: giving up on her, without ever exploring the middle ground, as messy as that might get. What about those odd moments of independence and lucidity I'd observed? What if she could do more than my father had thought? What about the day she'd summoned help? What about all the times she'd served me tea with milk?

Laura called back and said she could send caregivers to the house five or six days a week. Sundays were up to me, she said. This was major progress. All I had to do was figure out how to pay for it. My guess was that Barb didn't need long daily visits, just someone to check on her once a day, but CMSS couldn't afford to send caregivers for shifts of less than four hours at a time, so at six days a week for four-hour shifts, that meant I'd have to pay for twenty-four hours' worth of care a week. It wasn't going to be cheap. In the meantime, Laura said, she needed time to find the right person. The caregivers were accustomed to extreme physical illness, but mental illness was a different matter. It might take a while, she said. "Okay," I replied. My semester didn't start for a couple of weeks. Until we could get someone in place, I'd go every day.

Laura had been both practical and sympathetic when I admitted to her what I really wanted. In addition to a caregiver, I wanted to find someone to help Barb get better. What about psychiatric help? I wanted to know. Could Laura imagine that anyone would make a house call? She said she'd look into it, and here's where a little more organization would have come in handy. Three years earlier, Amy Smith had told us to call her when something changed. Now everything had changed, but I'd been in too much denial then to keep track of her and more recently too addled and scared and distracted by the immediate necessity of finding day-to-day help to remember her offer. But even though I'd forgotten about her, Amy planted the seed of hope that allowed me to believe there might be help out there when the time came.

A few days later, Laura called back. Good news, she said. One of her contacts had come up with the name of a private mental health agency in Northfield called Wilpower. She'd spoken with their outreach social worker, Wendy Trafny, who had agreed to talk with me. I called Wendy, and when I explained our situation, she agreed to come to the house to evaluate Barb. This was cause for celebration.

First, though, we had to get caregivers in place. Laura lined up Cheryl, a young nursing student with two small children. Cheryl and I talked on the phone, and she agreed to meet me at the house the following Tuesday with the intention of starting on Friday.

I typed up grocery lists, contact phone numbers, notes on the idiosyncrasies of the house including a detailed description of the laundry situation and what to do with the wet sheets and towels since there was no dryer—hang them on the clothesline in the basement until they stop dripping and then bring them up to hang on the shower rod where my sister would collect and fold them with exquisite care. It wasn't that she wouldn't do laundry—she washed most of her clothes by hand in the upstairs sink—she just wouldn't go into the basement. I drew a map to show Cheryl how to get to the nearest grocery store.

On Tuesday I arrived early to tidy up, although it wasn't necessary. Barb was compulsively neat. Then Cheryl arrived and I gave her a tour of the house. I called Barb to come out of the hall where she'd been standing, listening to us. I introduced them, and it was Barb who extended her hand gravely. "Hello," she said in a brave, weak impersonation of my father's heartiness. What was missing was my father's smile, but for Barb this greeting was a huge step.

Then we went outside so I could show Cheryl where to take the garbage and, once out of earshot of Barb, I gave her my cheery breezy sanitized version of Barb's condition. Barb was sweet, I told her. And, oh yes, she was also schizophrenic. Then I gave her one of the only four keys that opened the house, the master of which could not be duplicated at any lock shop—I had tried many—because it was so old and bent. The few copies we owned had been hand-tooled by a family friend in his machine shop. Cheryl left with my key and said she'd be back Friday.

On Friday Laura called to say that Cheryl couldn't start yet but would come Monday instead. On Monday Laura called to say that Cheryl had changed her mind and wouldn't be coming at all. After thinking it over she'd decided she didn't want to risk it. She had heard that schizophrenics were dangerous and she was afraid to be alone with Barb.

A few weeks earlier, I'd been channel surfing and seen part of a late night television movie in which a man and a woman are anxiously searching a house. Scary, suspenseful music plays in the background. The woman finds a bottle of pills and then, conveniently right next to it, a physicians desk reference. She holds up the pills to the camera, and we see her finger moving down the page as she looks up the name of the drug printed on the bottle. When the word on the bottle and the word on the page match, the camera moves to her face: horror! She runs out of the house and cries to her husband, "We have to get out of here! Now!" He is uncomprehending. "Wait, Linda," he says. "Not so fast. There must be some good reason Dave would do such a horrible thing." "Yes," she cries, holding up the bottle of pills. "*He's schizophrenic!*" The man's jaw drops. The scene ends as the camera zooms in for a close-up on their terrified faces. Then they turn and run.

So this is what we're up against, I thought. Schizophrenics were the new conscienceless movie monsters, on which all crime could be blamed, scarier even than aliens, zombies, and Nazis. I felt personally insulted, as if it were me Cheryl had refused to be alone with. The irony was that if anyone in the family was inclined to be dangerous right then, it was more likely to be me than my sister. And I wanted my key back.

Laura tried to soothe me. She told me not to be discouraged and reminded me again of what she, and everyone else, had told me before—this was uncharted territory. It could take a while to find the right person.

In the meantime, I went to the house every day. There was plenty to do. I cleared my father's old clothes out of the closets. I tried some on, and for a while I wore selected items around the house when I was there, forgetting to take them off when I left and wearing them home piece by odd piece. My dog got excited—I must have smelled like his dear old friend. His excitement made me sad. Some of the clothes were ancient and fell apart the first time I washed them. Even the ones that fit didn't really, though it hardly mattered; it was winter and I wore them in layers. I gave my father's neckties to Fritz. I salvaged the Harris tweed overcoat with the shredded lining and kept the white cotton shirt my brother had brought from the

Philippines thirty-five years earlier, the one with the fighting roosters embroidered on the front that my father wore for thirty-five summers in a row until—and after—it fell apart at the seams and a neighbor reconstructed it for him on her sewing machine. I felt an obligation to my father's clothes, to all the mended seams and the mismatched, sewn-back-on-by-him buttons. I felt an obligation to the memory of my father's monumental thrift to preserve these things, to not simply throw everything, which he had so carefully laundered, mended, folded, and stowed, out.

My sister, though, was not so sentimental. She kept urging me to purge, hanging around amiably during this process despite the fact that I usually stayed past her normal bedtime, which appeared to be around four o'clock in the afternoon. She brought me things she especially wanted me to throw away and thanked me profusely when I did. She rooted around in old kitchen cupboards I'd forgotten were there and produced bundles of half-century-old tea towels for disposal. Since she wouldn't leave the house, anything she wanted to get rid of had to be either sneaked out in the bottom of the wastebasket—a habit she'd developed under my father's watchful eye when he was trying to keep her from pitching the family silver—or, for larger items, negotiated out the door, now through me. I was the gateway to the garbage.

At first I resisted all this purging, but then I had a small epiphany. My sister's impulse to clean and clear was healthy. I was the one who was acting crazy now. So I got with the program and we went through boxes of garbage bags. I tried to interest her in taking some of my father's clothes but, except for the unopened package of long underwear Fritz had given him for Christmas the year before, which my father appeared to have been saving for a rainy day, she didn't want any of it, so we bagged it all for charity or the trash.

We organized stacks of suits, sweaters, stiff ancient shoes, bedding, old hospital supplies. She held the bags while I stuffed things in. I held the bags while she stuffed things in. It was mindless physical work, and I realized I was enjoying it. She seemed to be too. I kept thinking, so this is what it's like to have a sister. She was particularly adamant about wanting to get rid of the hospital supplies, which I'd stashed in a closet thinking I could donate to some cause. I held out for a while, but nobody would take the stuff and she wanted it out of the house. Finally, I pitched it. Why not? I thought. It's her house now.

When Tom was staying there after my father died, he bought Barb an electric keyboard, a Christmas present, to see if he could spark her interest. After he got back to Raleigh he'd dug out Anna's old practice books—Mozart, Chopin, Schubert, which she'd saved from childhood—and sent them to Barb. Now on one of my visits, in the bizarre, pitch-black dark of a late January afternoon, I set up the keyboard and struck a few chords. I tried to nudge her memory, encouraging her with my memories of her playing, but she would only just barely touch the keyboard, hitting a note or two and then backing away. She was interested in the sounds it made but didn't seem to remember how to play. Or didn't want to.

She was the one who'd played Chopin. I was the musically untalented one who quit piano lessons to take up violin and quit that too, but since she wouldn't play, I sat down on the floor in the deep darkness of the under-lit house when five o'clock feels like midnight and sounded out Christmas carols in the post-Christmas gloom. I plunked out all I could remember, *O Come All Ye Faithful*, *Joy to the World*, *Hark the Herald Angels Sing*. When I ran out of Christmas carols, I moved on to *Happy Birthday*, *Heart and Soul*, *Ode to Joy*, any melody I could remember well enough to pick out on the little keyboard while Barb stood by and smiled and even swayed a little with my horrible rhythm-less playing. I felt ridiculous but I was getting a reaction so I kept going, beyond embarrassment as Barb said approving things about my hideous two-fingered playing and moved to the music and laughed at my profanities when I missed a note and cheered me on, and when I finally found the note I was searching for, she called out, "You found it!" So, I thought again, this is what it feels like to have a sister.

February

A few weeks later, a group of old friends, women I'd known for twenty years, planned to gather at Beth's house for dinner. I badly wanted to go, badly wanted to sit around a table with a bunch of women and drink wine and eat chocolate cake and talk about something other than mental illness and death.

It was the coldest night of the year, one of those scarily cold February nights in Chicago when you wear four of everything and still can't get warm, when you wear your coat inside the house all day and try not to go out because you're afraid your car will break down by the side of the road and you'll freeze to death with an uncharged cell phone stuck to your head, one of those nights so cold that even my thick-skinned, heavy-coated, snow-loving dog has to be forcibly pushed out the back door to pee.

It was the first full week of daily caregivers, the first week I'd felt safe not going to the house every day, and I'd spent the afternoon in the city interviewing a sculptor at her studio. When I got home—with just enough time to change clothes and organize the food I planned to take to Beth's—there was a message from Laura saying there had been a mix-up. The caregiver scheduled for that day hadn't shown up. Which meant my sister had been alone all day.

I tried calling the house. Of course Barb didn't answer. It was already dark. I knew she was in bed. Or I hoped so. There was plenty of food, I knew, but that wasn't the point. What if the furnace shut off? Or blew up? What if the pipes burst? She wouldn't wear real shoes, only flip flops without socks—what if she wandered outside for some reason for the first time in thirty years? She'd never been alone there in the winter. I had no idea what she'd do.

It's February, I thought. I should go. It would take at least forty-five minutes to get there—the streets were icy—but if I left immediately and if everything there was okay, I could go on to Beth's afterward and arrive, if not in time for dinner, at least before everyone left. I knew I wouldn't, though. It was too cold, too icy, too much driving. I didn't have the energy. I had to choose.

I chose Beth's. I felt guilty about it—here I was enjoying life while my sister was alone on the coldest night of the year—and I worried the whole time, but I went.

After dinner, everyone started to talk about where they'd rather live. Jo said Chicago was too big. She wanted to go back to Michigan and raise horses. Linda, who'd grown up in Taipei, said Chicago wasn't big enough—she thought about moving to Shanghai. Mary wanted to go someplace warm, and Beth said she thought Paris would be nice. Then it was my turn. I shrugged and changed the subject. These conversations made me nervous. I didn't dare think about where I wanted to live. I didn't feel like I had a choice. I was tethered to my sister, poised for disaster at home.

· · · ◆ · · ·

Wendy came to the house for the first time on a cold February afternoon. I got there early to build a fire in the fireplace. I wanted to entice her any way I could, make her feel welcome so she'd want to come back. She'd made it clear on the phone with Laura and later with me that she couldn't promise anything. Like everyone else I'd talked to, she said she'd need to evaluate Barb before she could say whether it was safe for her to stay in the house alone.

It felt like an audition and I was nervous. I wanted Wendy to like us, and I wanted her to approve of this strange plan I was hatching. Then a green Honda came crunching up in the snow, and out climbed a woman about my age dressed in blue jeans with a short sporty haircut I admired. Toting a bulging briefcase, she stomped through the knee-high snow at the curb with an air of eminent practicality. She looked like she could be one of my friends.

We had agreed on the phone that I wouldn't give her the whole story then but would wait for Barb to tell it herself. I wanted to hear what Barb would say without prompting from me. So Wendy asked questions, and Barb told a version of her life story I'd never heard, leaving out almost everything since the early 1970s. I had to restrain myself from answering for her but, when I managed to, Barb spoke willingly, even expansively. She talked about her early memories of living in a tiny house on Grace Street, when she and Tom were small, and about her early married life in Lexi, as she called it. It seemed to be the time she remembered most happily, though she never mentioned Karim.

Later, after Barb retreated upstairs, I gave Wendy my version of things as we sat in the kitchen drinking tea. Wendy took notes and asked more questions. I waited nervously for her verdict, and when she said she wanted to watch and see what happened but thought for now that Barb could stay where she was with daily visits from caregivers, I was giddy with relief.

We'd done it. Barb had done it! Barb had risen to the occasion. She had been polite and engaged, answered questions at length, served grapes, even made jokes. She had not just cooperated, she'd charmed Wendy, asserting her personality in this first meeting more than I could remember having seen her do since she'd gotten back from Iraq. Partly, she seemed to understand that preserving her way of life now depended on her cooperation, although I hadn't told her that, but also she just seemed to enjoy talking with Wendy. And Wendy knew how to talk to Barb and, even better, how to listen, how to bring her out without scaring or condescending to her.

One of Wendy's questions for me was whether Barb had any insurance. I'd dug out the Social Security Insurance card from the very slim file that contained the record of our connection to the public aid system. Wendy said that was a start but that I'd have to get the legal guardianship papers and the SSI payments transferred to me as soon as possible, and she explained how to begin the process. What about her services? I wanted to know. Could she come back?

The situation was unusual, she said. In fact, in her twenty-five years as a social worker, she'd never seen anything quite like this. She visited Wilpower members in their homes all the time, she said, but more often they came to the office to see her, and for appointments with their psychiatrists and, mostly, for the sociability of the day program. But she could see that Barb wasn't ready for that yet—she'd asked and Barb had said no—so, okay, she said. She'd come to her. Say, once a week? "Wow," I said. And then, "How much will this cost?" Wendy shook her head. There would be no charge. Wilpower's services were covered by Barb's SSI.

It seemed too good to be true. Or as my father would have said, things were looking up.

From then on, Wendy came once a week. She gave me advice on what I could and couldn't expect from Barb, helped me to get things organized, told me who to call, where to go, which forms to fill out. There were a lot of forms to fill out. She asked Barb how she felt—"Oh, pretty good"—and asked me how I felt. I didn't know how to begin to answer such a question.

As she got ready to leave that first day, Wendy told me she thought Barb was adorable. *Adorable!* We'd passed a test, largely through Barb's effort, and I wanted to shout to someone, though I didn't know who—see, I *knew* she was adorable.

· · · ◆ · · ·

As Laura had predicted, it took a while to get the caregivers in place, but eventually we settled on a schedule with Lisa, who came every weekday, and Christine, who came on Saturday. Lisa was kind and resourceful and wrote long reports about her and Barb's activities on the yellow tablet I left on the dining room table. Christine was less communicative. My sister's only comment about her was that all she did was eat. One day, Barb refused to let her in.

Of all the problems I'd anticipated and despite Joyce's warning, here was one I hadn't even considered. I'd taken Barb's courteous and, up to now, somewhat passive nature for granted, but now she was expressing her opinions, and they weren't all positive. I hadn't figured on her actively disliking someone.

I had mixed feelings. I wanted her to like the caregivers and for them to like her, but if she was able to form and exercise opinions about their trustworthiness or friendliness—Christine didn't seem very friendly to me either—that was good, wasn't it? I talked to Laura and she said she'd look for someone else for Saturday. Then Lisa suddenly became unavailable too—a more lucrative job with longer hours had come along—and on her last day she left an open letter to her replacement on the yellow tablet asking that whomever took over for her "please take good care of Barbara as she is a sweet person." How could we lose someone like that?

But then in her place came Chantal, an intense young Haitian woman who spoke English in a deep-voiced French accent that immediately endeared her to my sister, as did her cooking, which consisted of a variety of spicy rice dishes with vegetables and yams. Best of all were her two little daughters whom she brought along when she couldn't find baby-sitters. It was against policy, but we all overlooked it. It made life easier for Chantal, and my sister clearly loved having them there.

Barb particularly liked when Chantal brought the younger of the two—a dark, square-faced two-year-old named Christal who regarded me with somber reserve the one time I met her but whom I could hear in the background when I called, romping, shrieking, and laughing as she tore around the house. Barb doted on her and reported on her doings—Christal jumped on the couch, Christal hid behind the curtains, Christal wore striped socks, Christal liked crackers. Here was a side of my sister I'd never seen—somewhere in those forty-some years since she'd sworn to me she wanted nothing to do with children, she'd come to love kids.

· · · ◆ · · ·

Every Friday, Wendy came to the house and asked my sister questions. Sometimes the answers didn't seem to make sense. Sometimes they made perfect sense.

Wendy, trying to talk Barb into going to the day program: Barb, does it bother you that you don't have friends?

Barb: You're my friend.

Though someone went to the house almost every day now, and though she assured me she liked living alone, I worried that Barb was lonely. If only she'd use the phone.

Fritz sometimes came with me on Sundays. After lunch—big spreads of deli food we'd set out on a tablecloth-covered card table in front of the fireplace to entice Barb to join us—we tried to get her to use the phone. Fritz would leave the room and call from his cell phone. Then I'd coach her to pick up, and he'd ask her what she wanted for lunch the next day. The following day, I'd show up with the food. I was trying to demonstrate cause and effect, but she didn't seem interested, didn't connect my food deliveries to the phone calls. When we persisted, she dismissed these exercises as games and said she didn't want to play anymore.

I gave up trying to get Barb to answer the phone and instead set it on speakerphone so it would broadcast the long chatty messages Tom and I took to leaving on alternating days. If Chantal was there when one of us called, she'd put Barb on and we'd talk about the weather.

I thought about money all the time. My father, at the advice of his lawyer, had eventually changed the will to make it more flexible, but I was still Barb's trustee and legal guardian, and I lay in bed every night unable to sleep, trying to add up columns of figures in my head that never quite added up. Somehow I had to pay caregivers to visit Barb six days a week or do it myself. Or they could go less often, which would save me money, and maybe she'd be okay, but then she'd be alone even more than she already was. And I couldn't control it anyway. Their lives were even more complicated than mine. One day they'd show up, the next they wouldn't. On the days they didn't show up, I liked not paying, but I didn't like her being alone, and I especially didn't like not knowing when they'd be there and when they wouldn't and which days I should go to fill in. Not that I could go every day unless I went at night, but what was the point of that since she'd be in bed by the time I got there? I could ask one of the neighbors to check on her in an emergency, but daily visits were something else.

As addled as I was by all this scheduling and as uncomfortable as the endless parade of strangers passing through the house made me—not Chantal and Lisa, but all the substitutes I'd never met—I had to admit that Barb was doing better. Everyone who'd even slightly known Barb before who saw her now agreed that she had improved remarkably in the weeks since my father had died, and it seemed like this had everything to do with the combination of her new social life and her new independence. It would be tricky to preserve and promote both without exposing ourselves to one wrong stranger, but it seemed like a risk worth taking if I could figure out how to pay for it.

And caregivers were only one of the expenses I spent my sleepless nights adding up. There were real estate taxes, food costs, utilities, landscapers in the spring, repairs. Who knew what the house would need? Already the plumbers had been back twice.

At least Wendy's visits were free. I could still hardly believe it, and she said she thought she might be able to find a psychiatrist willing to come to the house too. I told her my impossible dream— find someone to prescribe an antipsychotic. Wendy said it might, in fact, be possible. But she couldn't guarantee it. She couldn't guarantee anything because this wasn't like anything she'd seen before.

I worried that even if we could get a doctor to come to the house and prescribe something, Barb wouldn't take it. Wendy told me to buy vitamins to get her in the habit of taking a pill every day, so I bought an extra-large bottle of multivitamins. When I brought them over, afraid Barb would respond the way I knew my father would have—with suspicion if not violent opposition. Barb surprised me by liking the idea. I took one and she took one—no problem. I called the next day and asked if she'd taken her vitamin yet, and she said yes and asked me if I'd taken mine. For a while, I called every day when I knew Chantal was there and asked if she'd taken her vitamin. She always said yes. I asked Chantal to ask her, Tom to ask her. She started to get annoyed, but she always said yes, and then I started to worry she was lying just to please me. I tried to count the pills, but the bottle was huge and I lost count and couldn't be sure. Wendy brought over a weekly one day at a time pill container, and we filled it with seven vitamins, but Barb didn't like the container and wouldn't use it. I was losing patience and interest—I didn't give a damn about vitamins. I was worried she wouldn't take antipsychotics that I hadn't yet gotten anyone to prescribe.

I worried about money all the time. I had two accounts I was using for Barb's expenses, and both were dwindling. The largest payment by far went to the caregivers. I lost track of what account was for what and started to spend my own money—every time I shopped for myself I saw things she needed or might want—would strawberries brighten her life? Herbal shampoo? When I went to the grocery store for her, I saw things I needed. I felt like I spent half my life at the grocery store. Then I'd get to the house and see that the cash for the caregiver was depleted and leave my own. I was constantly anxious about money.

And about scheduling, which had everything to do with money. I tried to cut corners. I tried to coordinate Wendy's visits with the caregivers' days off. But it wasn't that easy. Sometimes Wendy needed to change days, sometimes the caregivers did.

Desperate, I emailed Laura and Wendy one morning, thinking that together the three of us might be able to figure something out. By three o'clock that afternoon, they were both at the house, Wendy trying to evaluate how much care Barb actually needed, and Laura trying to help me figure out a more affordable schedule. I hadn't planned it, but Barb, who clearly liked the company, showed up too. After all, the meeting was about her. So, remembering John's advice, I asked her what she thought. She said she didn't need someone to come every day. I wasn't sure I agreed, but I loved that she felt independent enough to say so.

Laura recommended considering other housing options— something my brother and I were talking about too—and said she knew of several nice places Barb might like. One was a former convent in the city that had been converted to studio apartments with common rooms and a dining hall. The total cost would be about the same as, maybe even less than, our current arrangement, and much less once we sold the house. I said I didn't know if Barb was ready or willing to make such a move, and then I realized she was standing in her usual spot in the corner, listening. I asked her what she wanted. She said she wanted to stay in the house.

The conversation wandered. I'd built a fire in the fireplace—it was yet another bitter cold day—and we lingered there, reminiscing about old TV shows. We named our favorites, sang theme songs. Barb hadn't spoken since she'd said she wanted to stay in the house. Then all of a sudden she said, "*Marcus Welby*. I like *Marcus Welby*."

Fritz had come along that day to help me shop for a new TV to replace my father's still marginally functional and highly unreliable old set. On our way over, we'd stopped at Best Buy and bought Barb a twenty-four-inch television with a built-in DVD player in less time than it usually took me to buy three bags of groceries. As Wendy, Laura, and I talked, Fritz installed the new TV, and by the time they'd left, he had it working.

For years we'd tried to talk my father into letting us replace his old TV, which only sometimes worked and often shut off in the middle of a program. For years, every time my brother visited, he'd threatened to pitch it and buy a new one, only backing down when my father raged and pleaded with him not to. Now we'd finally done it. Fritz, Barb, and I cheered the sleek silver thing that looked so out of place in the old house. Fritz showed Barb how to use the remote. When she pushed a button, the TV went on. When she pushed it again, it went off. More cheers. Perhaps life could be predictable after all. We were giddy. We'd smuggled contraband in behind the back of my father's still very present, eternally thrifty ghost, and when we left, Barb was sitting on the couch contentedly watching cartoons.

· · · ◆ · · ·

Within two days, Laura had gotten back to me with phone numbers for assisted care facilities. I made an appointment with the one she recommended, but I felt a little guilty. Barb had said she wanted to stay in the house.

Knowing that gave me a bargaining chip, though. I was starting to think that if we could get her to accept responsibility for having chosen to stay, maybe we could get her to compromise on some of the details. What if we got someone to live there with her in exchange for free rent? Barb might not like it, but she might be willing to put up with it if she understood why she had to. I didn't want to even think about forcing her to leave. I kept going in circles. Could we afford to keep her in the house? Could we get help paying for caregivers? Could we do a reverse mortgage? If we sold the house and moved her elsewhere, what could we even get for it? It was a teardown and the market was tanking.

Tom thought it was impractical to keep her there, and I knew he was right. I'd promised him I would at least go look at a few of the places Laura recommended. I was scared, though, afraid they would be sad, horrible, impossible, and foul smelling, that the bedrooms would be cramped and dark, the food disgusting, the common rooms too bleakly institutional, the other residents too bizarre.

Pulling up in front of Hartwell House, I felt immense relief. Here was the former convent Laura thought might suit Barb and, at least from the outside, I agreed. It looked genteel and homey, a well-maintained brick building on a corner in Andersonville. I knew the quiet leafy neighborhood well—twelve years before, I'd lived three blocks away and never noticed the place was anything other than a city apartment building rehabbed into upscale condos.

Inside was the same—simple but gracious. With its high ceilings and dark wood, the place felt less like a nursing home than it did a church. The former chapel had been converted into an exercise room. Pews were pushed against the walls to make room for treadmills; muted light filtered through stained glass windows. When I squinted up at the leaded glass I saw scenes from the lives of . . . nuns! My father's ten thousand get-thee-to-a-nunnery jokes rang in my ears. I imagined my sister's raucous laughter and made a mental note to point out the windows if I ever found myself touring her through the place. I suspected the proximity of stained glass to stationary bikes would strike her as funny as it did me.

We looked at bedrooms, inspected menus, talked about costs. I tried to picture Barb living there. It was an old people's home, but not everyone there was old. At sixty-three, Barb wouldn't even be the youngest. I wondered if they'd be nice to her, if they'd allow her harmless eccentricities, if they'd mind that she ate standing up or that she wandered around talking to herself. I wondered if she'd feel free to wander.

I pictured myself visiting her there, making friends with the other residents, bringing gifts, something for everyone so no one would feel left out. I tried to imagine her making friends. There were, after all, social opportunities, weekly visits from hairdressers, a lounge with a piano, an arts and crafts program—Barb might like that—a pleasant dining room with a posted menu that looked appetizing enough and, my guide pointed out, family parties on holidays. I imagined Fritz and me at the Fourth of July ice cream social or sitting through an early Thanksgiving dinner—paper turkeys hanging from the light fixtures, Fritz impatient to leave, annoyed at the blandness of the food. I imagined drinking pink champagne out of paper cups on Valentine's Day at a table decorated with an accordion-fold red paper heart.

It was a stretch. But it wasn't impossible. It wasn't even so bad. It was clean, quiet. It smelled good, like old wood and baking bread. The rooms were spacious, each with a private bath. I imagined moving Barb's new TV into her room. We passed the private mailboxes, and I thought of the home-baked cookies Tom's friend Sylvia had been sending to Barb, warm offerings that arrived on the porch on the coldest of days. I imagined them arriving here in one of these mailboxes and Barb sharing them with her new friends. A particularly golden fantasy that, the idea of her making friends, giving them cookies. On the way out I glanced at the weekly activities schedule—on Fridays they served wine and cheese. That was promising, I thought. At least they let them drink.

Moving her there would certainly be easier for me. I'd be able to leave town for more than a week at a time without having to worry about her. Or the caregivers. Or the groceries or the falling-down house or the bills or the schedule or the lawn or the furnace or the goddamned fucking plumbing. I could leave town whenever I liked, and for however long. I wanted to leave right then, drive straight to the airport and never come back. Maybe she'd like the place, I thought.

But. Could I do this to her? What bothered me wasn't the place itself, which in fact was nice, but that the people there were so clearly at the end of their days while my sister, though not exactly young, was, in her own way, starting over. It seemed like a good place to glide comfortably into death, but I wondered if it was any place to begin a new life. I wondered if moving her there would end all possibility of her ever finding her way back to herself.

Feeling encouraged, or at least open to considering what I had so long avoided, I drove to another place closer to home, a government-subsidized intermediate-care facility for mental patients. I hadn't made an appointment, but when I explained my situation, one of the social workers offered me a tour.

Here was another world, as noisy as the other place was silent. Here, everyone was younger and sicker, many visibly so, discussing their medications and hallucinations on the fly as we passed in the hallway. The place was crowded and crumbling, with creaky elevators, bad lighting, peeling paint, stale smells, and stacks of papers overflowing onto the floor in every office. Unlike the genteel privacy at Hartwell House, here everyone shared a room. It reminded me of a freshman dorm but at some nightmare college where the only course of study was the students' mental illness.

My guide, Caroline, trooped me up and down the halls. We peeked into activity rooms and bedrooms, chatted with some of the more outgoing residents. Caroline was unfailingly bright and kind.

The people I met were lively, purposeful, and friendly, though we also passed by dark rooms where I could see prone, still figures on beds, mumbling.

Caroline explained that all the residents were psychiatric patients and that most had come directly from hospitals. It was a move up for those who could handle the independence, she said. They were free to leave the premises and mingle in the community, free to visit local shops and businesses, including a nearby half-price movie theater, a bookstore, and the library. Whatever bad thoughts I'd had about the place disappeared when I thought of it in comparison to life in a psych ward, but it wouldn't be a move up for Barb, who had a house to herself and no interest in leaving it, especially to move to a place like this.

And as much as Barb needed to be around people—I'd figured that out by now—I couldn't imagine her there. It seemed like it would only make her worse. It would be free—all we'd have to do was sign over Barb's SSI payment—but it seemed like a last resort for someone who had nowhere else to go, not something we should do if we didn't have to. Better to sell the house and use the money to keep Barb at Hartwell, or someplace like it, indefinitely.

The next weekend, I went back to Hartwell with Fritz. I wanted a second opinion, and I knew he wouldn't bother to fake it if he thought it was awful. We toured the same half dozen bedrooms I'd seen the week before. He poked his head into each room to check the view and size up the best deal, tried out the beds and inspected the bathrooms like he was picking the best room at a country inn. He liked the place, he said. Someone even had a cat.

Afterward, feeling bolstered, we went on to another of Laura's recommendations, this one new and shiny, more like a business hotel than an old people's home, with a bank of elevators, a movie theater, and a gift shop in the lobby. We slipped past the receptionist and into an elevator, disembarked on a random floor where a well-coifed resident introduced herself and showed us her apartment. It was spacious, comfortable, and well appointed, but it didn't feel right for Barb.

I couldn't imagine her feeling at home there, negotiating the modern glass-walled elevators, pushing the right buttons, getting off on the right floor, finding her own room, chatting with the well-coifed lady without freaking her out, not feeling "afeared," as she called it. We left, exhausted.

The next day was Sunday. I had paperwork to do at the house, and Fritz came along to keep me company. We brought food—lox and bagels, corned beef sandwiches, cinnamon rolls—also a bottle of wine, a load of firewood, a newspaper, a movie. I was operating on instinct. Maybe creature comforts would help. Make it a party, see what happens.

Noticing Barb's interest in cartoons, Fritz had bought her a DVD of *The Little Mermaid,* and after lunch we sat down to watch it. Or at least Fritz and I sat. Barb stood in her usual spot in the corner, smiling at the songs and commenting on the experience if not exactly on the movie itself.

Barb: We are biological freaks.

Me: What? Why?

Barb: We want to be children, but we are not.

Pretty soon, she started to wander, up and down the stairs, in and out of the room, conferring in private with her phantom voices.

Fritz fell asleep on the couch. Barb came and went. I started to wander the house too, searching for something, though I didn't know what. Family history, a mildewed letter explaining everything shoved between the pages of an old book, art maybe. There was a stack of paintings in the basement, wrapped in brown paper, covered with decades-old layers of undisturbed dust. I unwrapped each one, hoping for treasure, something to take home, a sentimental Victorian dog portrait, maybe, the likeness of some dour ancestor, but nothing there was anything I wanted.

The house was full of relics, things left behind, other people's cast-offs. In an upstairs closet, in my old bedroom, hung my sister's forty-year-old wedding dress, still in its plastic bag. The room had been her girlhood bedroom. The night she took the dress off, the room became mine. I'd occupied it for six years, until I went away to college, and the whole time the dress hung there, its voluminous presence, in its plastic garment bag, haunting the back of my not-large closet like a bulky ghost. I never removed it, never felt I had the right to. I never even unzipped the bag all the way, afraid that if I did, that shining white dress would engulf me somehow, smother me with its lingering scent of sweat and expectation and Chanel No. 5.

Barb appeared to have forgotten the dress, which she'd never cared much about to begin with, and that afternoon seemed like a good time to pitch it. Or at least donate it to some charity thrift store. Who knew what imaginative use some art student might find for a size four, slightly used 1966 wedding dress? But it was too big to smuggle out of the house without my sister noticing. I'd have to explain or at least ask permission as I dashed past her out the door with it. I didn't think she'd object—I just didn't feel like having the conversation.

I closed the closet door and wandered back to the basement. I wanted the house to give something up—to me. It was venal, I knew, but I felt like it owed me. All my life I'd had dreams about that basement. Once I dreamt I'd found a silver violin in a purple lined case there. I knew it was a pregnant metaphor, a barely disguised symbol for my family's history, our secrets, our past, our buried possibilities, but the basement was also full of real, physical stuff. I kept hoping it would yield up some rare, exquisite, life-changing thing just for me. I returned to it year after year, expecting its contents to change, as they had when I was a child as people died or moved away and their stuff was added, like sediment, to the piles already there. But the only new additions I found that day, as Fritz dozed and Barb fretted upstairs, were a few dead mice.

Later, as we were leaving, Barb asked me to buy her scotch tape and forks. Then in another, deeper voice she said, "You are a spoiled brat." She didn't seem to be addressing me, and I couldn't be sure, but it appeared that a voice in her head had spoken out loud this time and was telling her she was a spoiled brat for asking for scotch tape. I'd never heard the voice, but now that I had, I didn't like it. I didn't like it at all. The voice was now my enemy too. I made a mental note to buy her a mountain of tape.

····◆····

The next day, Monday, was the monthly meeting of Wilpower's family support group. I'd promised to go, at least once. Part of me wanted to; meeting other people in our situation was something I'd imagined doing. But another part of me was keeping score. This would be the fourth day in a row devoted to Barb. I resented that arranging for her care was becoming the center of my life.

The meeting was scheduled for 6:00 p.m. at the Wilpower offices, and I arrived early, not knowing what to expect. Two Wilpower peer counselors were scheduled to speak but, until they stood up to talk, I couldn't pick them out from the dozen or so ordinary-looking people who sat in a circle in the dayroom.

Bill went first. He was a nervous man, in his forties or early fifties, serious, intense, sincere. He said it was hard to hold a job, described his many hospitalizations. He talked about his meds, their side effects and his not-always-sympathetic family. Then, with the same matter-of-factness that he spoke about his sister and mother, he started to talk about his voices. It was the first time I'd ever heard anyone admit they heard voices. The few times I'd asked Barb, she'd denied it and I didn't press. It seemed too private. Bill, though shy and anxious, spoke openly about them. He knew they were a symptom, he said, but he still wasn't always sure they weren't real when he heard them.

Then Joe stood up to speak. I might have figured out that Bill was schizophrenic if I'd watched him long enough—he seemed uncomfortable, didn't make eye contact. But Joe was the last person in the room I would have guessed was sick. He was self-composed, handsome, well dressed, articulate, and completely comfortable in front of a group. He could have been a salesman or a teacher.

Like any good speaker, he told stories. Horror stories. At six, he'd heard voices speaking to him from a turned-off television set. As a teenager, the voices got so loud he drank and took drugs to drown them out, but couldn't. He couldn't go to college, couldn't concentrate, couldn't hold a job. He holed up in his parents' basement. By the time he was in his mid-twenties, the disease was full-blown. A voice told him to sacrifice his cat. At the worst of it, one Good Friday, in a religious frenzy, he'd driven a six-inch nail through the palm of his hand. His survival, he said, hinged on the moment he'd agreed to medication.

I learned that night how it feels to be schizophrenic. I thought I knew, from watching Barb, but these men stood in front of a group and described it. They said it was lonely. They said it was terrifying. Weird, intrusive thoughts kept them from feeling comfortable around other people. They couldn't distinguish their symptoms from reality.

A third man I'd assumed was a supportive parent or sibling, who turned out to be another schizophrenic, agreed. He said he'd once mistaken the taunting voices in his head for real ones and run up and down the hall of his apartment building banging on doors, demanding to know who was yelling obscenities at him. The other two men nodded. It wasn't news to them.

But it was to me, all of it. Bill had had electric shock therapy; Joe had gained and lost hundreds of pounds, a side effect of medication. They'd endured multiple hospitalizations, estrangement from family, broken romances, lost jobs, depression, suicide attempts. Yet here they were, working, living on their own. Joe had a girlfriend. These were some of the bravest people I'd ever met.

The meeting wasn't particularly well attended, and afterward everyone drifted off as if nothing special had happened. But for me it had. Here was incontrovertible evidence of what I'd always hoped might be possible for Barb. Here were people who'd been at least as sick as, maybe sicker than, she was—I couldn't stop thinking about the six-inch nail—who now lived independent, productive lives. They talked about their psychiatric symptoms the way other people talked about their physical health. Schizophrenia was a problem they lived with, and though it was sometimes grave and discouraging, it was not the single defining condition of their lives.

And what they'd said about their symptoms confirmed everything I'd observed in Barb. It seemed like she too heard mocking echoes of her own voice. Her life too was constricted by fears others thought were foolish. She was *afeared* of violent photos on a magazine cover, *afeared* to go into the basement, *afeared* to leave the house, take a walk, or even to go onto the porch. When I asked her to get the newspaper off the front steps, she said no. When I asked why, she said she was *afeared* to lean. The difference between these men and Barb was that Barb believed she had to keep it all a secret.

The men who spoke that night were younger than Barb, and they'd all been on meds for years, but still I wondered. If they could go from being as sick as they'd described to speaking in public and holding jobs, why couldn't Barb change too?

·····◆·····

Wendy came to the house once a week. At first she'd tried to talk Barb into coming to see her—there was a bus that collected Wilpower members at their homes and brought them in for day programs—but backed off when Barb continued to refuse. So when I told Wendy about Hartwell House on her next visit and asked what she thought about moving Barb there, she said she thought it was a little premature.

I'd been hoping she might see it differently, but I knew she was right. It put me back to where I'd been—trying to figure out how to keep Barb in the house.

At least there were small improvements. That week Barb let Wendy give her a hug.

It was another of those small things that was huge for us. Barb had begun to tolerate being touched. In particular she liked Wendy, who was nonthreatening and matter-of-fact. She asked Barb questions no one else had dared to and then listened to the answers and didn't try to talk Barb out of her positions, even when they were strange or not what we wanted to hear. Barb became her most charming self around Wendy, making quips, telling stories, and taking special care with her clothes and hair on the days she knew Wendy would visit. Fritz wondered half jokingly if Barb had inherited a genetic predisposition for charm from my father. Charm as a genetic endowment strong enough to overpower the voices for a while? Why not? I thought. Though why not before? Whatever the cause, though, after all those years of shrinking away, Barb was starting to open up.

Since she wouldn't go out into the world, we tried to bring it to her. Tom started sending DVDs. *Groundhog Day*, *Titanic*, yoga lessons, dance lessons, *Sesame Street* movies. On Sundays we'd pick one and watch it. Chantal's kids had turned Barb into a *Sesame Street* fan, and a Kermit the Frog movie Tom sent quickly became her favorite. As she had with *The Little Mermaid*, Barb paid more attention to the visuals and the soundtrack than she did to the plot. Standing at a safe distance in the hallway, she wondered who had composed the score and commented on the stylishness of Kermit's eyeglasses.

I had streamlined my visits to two days a week by then, but Chantal called me almost daily to report on the details of Barb's life, her viewing habits, her diet, her vitamins. She got Barb to drink milk by making hot cocoa with cinnamon and vanilla. She got her to eat vegetables. On the days Chantal brought her daughter, the little girl ran to the stairs and called Barb's name—Bar-by!—and Barb came downstairs to greet her. Chantal told me that Barb had offered to babysit when she went out to shop.

Barb particularly liked the newspaper. At first, I couldn't tell if she read it or just wanted the familiar ritual of leafing through it every day. She'd look at the pictures and the ads and point out ones she especially liked. "Oh look, *a baby!* Cute!" she'd say, or "Look! *A kitten!*" Or she'd show me something in a glossy ad insert and nod knowingly. "Expensive!" she'd say. *Expensive* was her all-inclusive default term of admiration, second only to *cute,* and she applied it to everything from fingernail files to sports cars.

But then she began telling me about what she'd read. One day, with the same intense interest she'd exhibited toward the kitten photo, she asked me if I'd seen the article about strangulation. A man had strangled his wife, she said pleasantly, nodding and smiling. I said no, I hadn't seen it. I wondered if it was even real since the violent content so closely matched what I often overheard her discussing with her voices. But when I looked it up in that day's newspaper, there was the story, on page seven of the *Chicago Sun-Times.*

When I finished reading it out loud, she smiled brightly and said, "He strangled her for the insurance money." It was pretty much true, or rather because he'd found out he wouldn't get the money— the victim had refused to name her husband as beneficiary, so he killed her. What got my attention wasn't even that Barb seemed to grasp the weirdly spiteful and self-defeating nature of the crime but that she saw the humor in it. Then she served me pound cake and tea—by then she regularly waited on me like some old-fashioned hostess—and suggested we turn on the news to see what other crimes were being committed.

As if she'd planned it, there on local TV was live coverage of a domestic shooting in the next suburb, not five miles away. The shooter had barricaded himself in his house, which, as we watched in real time, was surrounded by a SWAT team. I had driven within blocks of the crime scene on my way over, half an hour earlier.

It was an eerie coincidence, one of many in which Barb seemed connected to things she had no way of knowing, and eerie also that she felt especially connected to violent crime. I worried the news report would make her even more fearful—she lived alone, the murder scene was nearby—but she watched calmly, cheerfully even. She was full of fears about obscure dangers that were hard for me to understand—why fear leaning?—but when it came to the murderer three miles away, she was unconcerned. Maybe, I thought, it was reassuring. Maybe it gave her a sense of reality to know that these violent scenarios that were so much on her mind did in fact happen in the real world.

By late February Barb was making more choices, had begun voicing opinions about the house. She arranged books and magazines in rigid stacks. If I bumped one out of order, she rushed over to right it. She complained that one of the caregivers had "demoted" her when she'd moved the family photos on the mantle to dust them. She cleaned and organized and threw things out—food, clothes, the occasional sterling silver fork. She wanted me to throw out the mahogany desk chair. I resisted. That seemed to be going too far. Though the seat was sprung, it had been Grammy's and it was a good piece.

I suggested re-caning it. She said no and pointed at the chipped veneer. She'd always been attuned to visual detail and was more so now than ever. She took care in how she tied her scarves, in the artful way she served food. She cut her own hair and somehow managed to get it even all the way around the back. When I arrived looking askew, she straightened my clothes, brushed cat hair off my lapel. I understood—the chipped veneer bothered her.

We negotiated a compromise. We would put the keyboard on the chair, covering the broken seat and obscuring the chip. I'd take the good chair, which the keyboard had been resting on, back upstairs. She said, "Oh no, it's too much for you to carry," and I said, "No, it's fine." So I took the chair upstairs, and she was pleased. This was progress. Not only was she expressing opinions, she was revealing herself to be a good negotiator.

Barb was emerging from her shell, beginning to take charge of her environment. Certainly she was very ill, but maybe her withdrawal hadn't only been a result of her disease, I thought. Maybe, partly, it was something more basic, a response to not having had any privacy, any say over the conditions of her adult life. My father had taken care of her, but he'd also ruled over her, controlling every detail of their life together. It seemed more and more obvious that the key to her recovery, as much as anything else, would be for us to honor any reasonable choices she made.

At first I worried it wouldn't work. I'd suggested she make out a grocery list, but I was afraid she'd ask for expensive or outlandishly hard-to-procure items or huge quantities. I was remembering the Charlie perfume story. But she didn't. On any given day, she wanted nothing more exotic than two tomatoes, vanilla ice cream, and a loaf of bread. When she wrote French mustard on her list, I bought her Dijon, and she said thank you but she'd meant French's brand.

She revealed herself to be cost conscious. She asked me to turn off lights to save electricity. She recycled plastic bags. The extent of my sister's extravagance turned out to be brand loyalty—she wanted Hellmann's mayonnaise and preferred the slightly more expensive Bays English muffins over Thomas', but then, who didn't?

· · · ◆ · · ·

One day toward the end of February, I took Barb chili and cornbread, planning to spend the day. I had work to do there. I paid the week's bills. I checked the vacuum cleaner for problems—Chantal said it wasn't working again—sorted the mail, picked up phone messages—people were still calling my father—replenished the cash for the caregivers. As usual, much of what was on my list had to do with money—balancing the checkbook, paying the bills, making sure there was enough cash in the small stash for groceries and other necessities.

At first I'd worried about leaving cash. Though it wasn't much, it seemed like a potential flashpoint in our relationship. I controlled the money, and I didn't want that to make her feel excluded or overruled. What would she feel about my routinely taking money out of my wallet and putting it somewhere for someone else to use? Would she want it for herself, would she want more than what I left? Should I explain to her why I left the amount I left and not more? What did money mean to her? Did she feel I was controlling her through extravagance, through stinginess? Should I give the money to her to give to them? What if she threw it out or tore it up as she sometimes did with the mail? But it turned out to be one thing I didn't need to worry about. While she often remarked that things were *expensive,* she was completely uninterested in actual cash.

While I worked, she made me tea—routine by now, but it still delighted me—then said, "Do you want to watch TV?" I said, "What about a movie?" And she said, "Sure."

We got out all the movies Tom had sent, and she chose *Titanic.* Though she wouldn't sit down or even stand still and kept leaving the room to go upstairs and mumble with her voices, she seemed interested and returned to hover on the stairs and listen. As usual, she didn't follow the plot exactly, and when I asked her if it was scary—it was to me—she said no. Instead she focused on the characters' appearances, admiring their opulent clothes and elaborate hairstyles. When Rose appeared as a beautiful one-hundred-year-old, she commented, "Now that's a cute old bag."

Midway through, she suggested we turn on the news, but later she seemed to still be thinking about the movie.

Me, sneezing: I have a cold.

Barb: Do you suppose you caught it from the iceberg?

····◆····

There was a never-ending list of details and problems to be taken care of at the house. Things clogged, cracked, failed, wore out, ran out, broke down. Light bulbs needed changing. Meters needed reading, vacuum cleaner bags needed replacing. Two days after we'd watched *Titanic*, Chantal called to say they were having plumbing problems again. As an afterthought, she mentioned that Barb had received some official-looking piece of mail, which she had torn up and thrown away.

I asked Chantal to retrieve it from the garbage and read it to me over the phone. It was a letter announcing that Wendy's request for additional aid for Barb had been denied due to a failure to reply to a previous letter. I was trying to transfer all official correspondence to my home address, but in the meantime who knew what important documents were disappearing into the wastebasket along with unwanted food and what little remained of the family silver?

March 1

March 1 was the big day. Dr. Weinstein, the Wilpower psychiatrist, was coming to see Barb. From my first conversation with Wendy I'd expressed my wish—which felt like just that, some flimsy longing in the form of fairy dust sprinkling through the night sky—that Barb see a psychiatrist. A psychiatrist, that is, who'd be willing to make a house call. And prescribe medication. Wendy promised nothing but quietly went to work on the project and by late February announced she'd found a doctor willing to come to the house. An appointment was set for Thursday, March 1 at three o'clock in the afternoon.

I canceled my Thursday afternoon class as soon as Wendy told me that was the only time Dr. Weinstein could make it. The first-ever visit from a psychiatrist was not something I could abandon Barb to without support, nor an event I planned to miss.

So with no class that Thursday I had the whole day to devote to Barb. And the house. First I went shopping for vacuum cleaner bags, then to buy groceries. I got there early to pay bills and after that I went to work on the kitchen sink, the woes of which I'd listened to my father lament for most of my life—hundred-year-old house, tree roots, original plumbing. Now I wished I'd listened better. I knew I needed to call a professional but thought maybe I could at least empty the sink of standing water.

Barb brought me the plunger and stood nearby while I pumped it up and down, clumsily at first, then more confidently as I worked up a sweat. What the hell, I thought—anything was possible. If a psychiatrist could make a house call, maybe I could fix a sink. Barb cheered along with me when finally, incredibly, it drained. Victory. I wasn't very good at this sort of thing—at home Fritz would have done it—but everything about this day felt lucky to me, and Barb felt it too. We high-fived. "Wow," she said. "Women's lib!"

It was another bitter cold day. I built a fire in the fireplace. At 2:55 I lit it. Then, a little after 3:00, two cars pulled up in the snow outside. Dr. Weinstein and Wendy had arrived.

Wendy had advised me to remind Barb they were coming and to make it clear that Dr. Weinstein was a psychiatrist. I'd waited until the last minute, until it was too late to cancel, thinking the less time she had to dread it the better, and her response—a predictable combination of fear and irritation telegraphed in unmistakable family body language—wasn't promising. Now the psychiatrist was standing on the front porch and I was afraid she'd flee upstairs as soon as we got past the pleasantries.

But, she didn't. Once again, Barb rose to the occasion, initiating a tense but polite handshake at the door and staying downstairs the whole time. She alternated between sitting and standing, poised to flee if necessary, but never actually left the room except for a few forays into the kitchen for grapes, which she politely offered around. Once she realized the doctor wasn't going to hurt her, she relaxed and even seemed to enjoy the sociability, showing flashes of the witty old Barb.

What made it all possible was the thing I wished my father could have lived to see, both to please him and to prove him wrong. Dr. Weinstein was a nice guy. Kind. Unintimidating. Nonthreatening. Low key. Polite. Gentle. Respectful. He acted as if he were there to ask my sister a favor, and the favor was that she simply talk to him. Barb, gracious by nature, responded by granting it.

He asked her lots of questions, slowly, in a quiet voice, and then listened to her answers and took notes openly. He asked her about the photos on the mantle, asked who the people were and how she felt about them. He asked if she ever felt depressed or suicidal. Yes, she said, sometimes she did. He asked about her childhood, her education. He asked if she was in pain—sometimes, she said—about what food she liked and how her appetite was. He asked her age and she told him she was forty-seven. He looked at me. I said she was born in 1943. He nodded and wrote something down. He asked if she heard voices and she said no, but later she told him what "they" were telling her. She talked about her fears and theories—gas attacks, biogenetics, the military industrial complex—and he listened. When he admired the photo of my mother on the buffet—a 1940s-style glamour shot taken before she was married—and asked who that beautiful woman was, Barb said it was "an impersonator of the mother." He asked her if she was sad about Dad and she said no.

As she relaxed she began to be funny, riffing on his careful language and teasing him when he said he was from Wilpower. "Wilpower? You're from Will Power? Oh, come on!" It reminded me of the first time she'd met Wendy when she'd replied to some simple question, the answer to which was no, by rattling off a list of approximate and increasingly imaginative synonyms—some rhyming—and ending triumphantly in "Zed!"

During one of Barb's trips to the kitchen to get grapes, Dr. Weinstein spoke to me. He said Barb seemed to be paranoid schizophrenic. He suggested we try to get her to come to the office—he didn't normally go to see patients in their homes, he said. None of his colleagues did either. I said I knew that, and thanked him again for making an exception for us, but that she wouldn't leave the house. And then, thinking this might be my only chance, I asked him if he would prescribe something.

He hesitated. I held my breath. He said he hadn't even brought his prescription pad into the house. "But, well, okay. Let's try something," he said. Then he put on his coat, went out to his car to get his pad, came back in, and wrote a three-month prescription for a daily dose of 0.25 mg of Risperdal.

Risperdal is an antipsychotic given to Alzheimer's patients and ADD kids, he explained. It helped focus their thoughts. He'd prescribed a child-sized dose. Even so, there might be some side effects, he said. Tiredness and stiffness were likely. Weight gain was possible. But the extremely low dose was intended to keep those to a minimum. There might be a psychiatric nurse who'd be willing to come to the house to check on Barb between his visits, he said—*Visits! He was coming back!*—and in the meantime, Wendy could monitor Barb's progress. He said the medication should quiet the voices if not totally silence them and give her some peace with her own thoughts.

By this time Barb had returned from the kitchen and was listening carefully so Dr. Weinstein spoke to her as he handed me the prescription. "We're going to try a very low dose to start with," he told her, "because you are so petite. And because you're new to drugs, and," he said, gently, "because you are in your late forty-sevens."

After Dr. Weinstein left, Wendy called the prescription in to Wilpower's pharmacy. They were nearby, still open, and kept antipsychotics in stock. If I hurried I could pick up the pills and get back in time for Barb to start taking them that night.

So off I went, on another rush into the darkening winter afternoon to buy drugs. In November it had been morphine for my father. Now it was antipsychotics for Barb.

The pharmacist was a kindly, avuncular man whose bushy mustache, white smock, and sweet matter-of-factness were straight out of a Norman Rockwell painting. He managed to verify online that Barb qualified for public aid even though I hadn't been able to find her current MediPlan card—apparently she'd pitched that too—and showed me how the dated, easy-to-use blister pack was designed to help patients organize their pill-taking. Then, without ceremony, he handed me a month's supply of Risperdal. My hands shook as I pulled out my wallet. I waited to hear what I owed, so grateful I almost didn't care what it cost, but he frowned when I handed him my credit card and shook his head. "All covered," he said. "Medicaid." The pills were free.

By the time I got back to the house it was late and dark, past Barb's usual bedtime, but she was up, waiting for me.

"Look," I said. "I brought you some things." Before I'd left I'd asked if she wanted anything else from the drugstore, to soften the singular importance of the pills, and the things she'd requested were in the bag with the Risperdal.

She shook the items onto the kitchen table, remarked approvingly on the Band-Aids, and then picked up the pill card. She was interested in the packaging. I explained how to take them, one a day according to the dates on the back, how to push the plastic blister against the pill and then push the pill through the flimsy paper backing. I explained she had to take one pill every night before she went to bed and she nodded. She read everything on the package out loud—"Oh, 0.25 milligrams," she said. "Take at bedtime." Then she said, "Do I punch it out like this?" and without further ado or any encouragement from me she punched out the pill for March 1, popped it in her mouth, and swallowed.

I'd been waiting thirty years for her to take that pill. And for as long as I'd anticipated it I'd dreaded that when the time came she wouldn't do it. But she did, willingly and happily. Almost eagerly.

Then she collected her things to carry upstairs—the little piece of paper with the days of the week written on it in neat columns that she carried with her at all times, the pharmacy bag, the box of Band-Aids, and the pill card on the bottom, all stacked neatly in order of size like schoolbooks—and announced she was going to bed. She walked halfway up the stairs, paused on the landing to turn in my direction, smiled more broadly than I'd seen her smile in many years, and blew me a kiss.

March 2–31

The next time I went to the house, three days later, there was still only one pill missing. Barb had skipped two days, even though I'd called both days to remind her to take her pill and to remind Chantal to remind her. I was upset, and she could tell. I explained how important they were, though vaguely, since she didn't acknowledge the symptoms they were meant to control. I asked her to please take them, every single day, like vitamins. Then before I left, I checked again—for some reason I knew I should—and now four pills were gone. She'd taken three while I was there. I tried to stay calm. I didn't want to confuse or scare her and I was touched that she was trying to cooperate. But now I was afraid she would overdose herself.

It was Sunday afternoon. Early the next morning I contacted Wendy, who called the doctor. He emailed back that he didn't think it was a problem. The dose was very low, he said. She would just be drowsy and stiff. I called Deborah, that day's caregiver and a regular substitute I'd grown to trust, and she said that Barb looked a little sleepy but otherwise seemed fine. I asked her to check the pills and she said five were gone. That meant Barb had taken one on her own that day, without my prompting.

But this meant I had to keep track, maybe indefinitely. I had to figure out how to get Barb to take one pill and only one pill every day. Tom and I started calling daily to remind her, asking Chantal to check her pills or getting her to put Barb on the phone so we could ask her if she'd taken her pill. When I was at the house I asked her to bring me the pill card so I could count how many she'd taken. At first Barb was cooperative, bringing me the package and standing there while I counted, but it made me feel like a cop and she didn't like being policed. Pretty soon she began to hide the pills, stashing them in various drawers and cubby holes around the house, moving them to a different place every few days, hiding them in her underwear drawer or under stacks of books, maybe to keep some part of her life private or just to keep us from haranguing her though the more she hid them the more we bothered her. Some days no pills would be gone, on other days several at a time. The more irregular her pill taking became the more tense I got and the more I asked her about it and the more she hid them.

When I complained to Wendy, she put it in perspective. We were lucky, she said. Barb was forgetful sometimes—although hopefully as the Risperdal took effect her mind would clear—but at least she wasn't resistant to medication, as so many patients were. If anything, she was over-taking it.

Wendy was right. It made me wonder if this meant what it seemed to mean, that despite her decades-long denial, Barb wanted help.

I also wondered about the ethics of not discussing with Barb the nature of the pills I was so urgently pressing on her. Though Dr. Weinstein had told her exactly what they were when he prescribed them, I didn't want to labor the point, didn't want to give her the chance to refuse them until they started to work.

She never did. She forgot them sometimes but never refused to take them, never even questioned them. She seemed to think of them as another kind of vitamin. Sometimes she asked me if I took vitamins too. Yes, I said and then went home and took one so it would be true. I wanted her to understand the pills as something she took to help her stay well, not something that meant she was sick.

Even though she clearly wanted to take the pills, she didn't see herself as ill. Once, when Wendy described to me another of her clients, I noticed Barb listening closely. She seemed to want some explanation, so I said, "Wendy is telling us about people she knows who have a schizophrenic son." Barb shook her head and said, "Oh, how sad," but she didn't seem to connect the story to herself or to Wendy's visits.

In the days after Dr. Weinstein's visit, I waited for results, or side effects, or something, anything, to happen, though I'd been warned not to get my hopes up. One possible, even probable, outcome, I'd been told, was that nothing at all would change.

March 6: Day 6

She already sounds better. I called this morning and got Chantal, who confirmed that the pills were all punched out for every day and said she would remind Barb to take one before she left. She put Barb on the phone. Barb sounded more cogent. She asked me how I liked the snow. She described the "child socks" Chantal's daughter was wearing and when I asked her to promise she would take her pills she said loudly, "I promise!" She sounded like she meant it.

Within days, Barb was calmer, more focused. She stood up straighter. She smiled more, made eye contact when we spoke. She seemed more able to listen, less distracted. Her responses were more related to what I said. She retreated less. She even seemed to speak less to her voices.

March 9: Day 9

Barb is definitely different. She's brighter, more engaged, better able to follow conversation. Wendy says so too. She didn't think the drug would work that fast but Maria Moreno, the psychiatric nurse who came to the house today, says that it does, that it can take effect sometimes within twenty-four hours.

Wendy and Maria stayed for almost two hours that day and Barb remained downstairs the whole time. She was more focused and engaged than I'd seen her in decades, joining in as we admired her new TV, talking about old TV shows from the 1960s. Maria asked Barb about her physical health but also wanted to know about her interests. Barb told her she'd liked to sew. She made jokes. She even let Maria check her blood pressure and heart rate. It was her first checkup since 1975 and involved a level of trust and physical contact with a stranger that hadn't seemed possible even a few weeks before. Partly it was the people—Maria, like Wendy, was warm and sensitive and enormously respectful of Barb and our situation—but it also had to be the drugs. Barb seemed to recognize and appreciate the change too. When Maria got up to leave, Barb shook her hand and told her, "You do good work."

March 11: Day 11

I go to see Barb—it's Sunday—I'm eager to see how she'll be after our extraordinary Friday but when I get there she's mumbling to herself and seems preoccupied. I'm disappointed. She's worse than she was just two days ago. I check her pills but she's up to date so that's not it. Maybe she needs more. Now that she's responding to Risperdal I want to up the dose.

We watch *Phantom of the Opera,* another movie Tom sent. She seems to focus better but, as she did with *Titanic,* responds to the music, the fancy clothes, and the lavish surroundings more than she does to the plot and wants to turn it off midway through to watch TV.

Barb likes TV. I wonder if it's because the quick changes and violent content match her thoughts, or if news and cartoons—her two favorites—provide a crash course in what's happening in the world. Or maybe she likes it because it blocks the sound of her voices. She especially likes *Dora the Explorer.*

March 16: Day 16

Friday. I meet Wendy at the house for our standing meeting. Barb is back to being focused and engaged. She listens to our conversation and joins in when she has something to add. I say I had a dream about Dad and she says sometimes she dreams about driving. "I'm even driving," she says, acknowledging how long it's been. Then she reminisces about her cars—the Malibu in Lexington, the Peugeot in Basra.

At one point she interrupts me to say something about Barbra Streisand and then says, "Oh, I'm sorry. I broke into your story." It was ordinary courtesy. She was self-assured enough to interject what she knew was an interesting comment and polite enough to direct the conversation back to the original topic afterward. It's been a very long time since I've seen her operate at this level of social ease and grace. It's like she's waking up, becoming herself again.

After Wendy leaves I sit down on the little couch in the hall to make a phone call. Barb sits down next to me. She hasn't sat next to me, close enough to brush shoulders, in years and years. Usually she stands, cowers almost or, when she rarely sits in anyone's presence, does so tensely and at a safe distance. This afternoon, though, she just sits next to me as if it's nothing special to seek out a little human contact. The sudden capricious companionability of it reminds me of my cat. I am astonished. I am grateful. I sit very still.

In mid-March, during my semester break, Fritz and I took a five-day vacation. Tom agreed to call Barb every day; Deb offered to back him up. I gave them each other's phone numbers and gave Tom numbers for Wendy and Laura. The idea was that everyone would remind Barb to take her pills, and that Tom and Deb would make sure the caregivers were there and summon help if they weren't. I needed a break.

We left Thursday morning and got back Monday night. On Tuesday evening I went to see Barb. I arrived around 6:00 p.m., late for her. I could tell she'd been asleep, but even as she began to wake up she was vague and disconnected. I gave her some things I'd brought from the trip, checked the mail, inventoried the groceries, and then checked her pill pack. She hadn't taken a single pill while I was gone.

I felt a spike of anger, then immediately guilt. I'd just spent five days in the Caribbean. But why this sudden relapse? Tom had reminded her daily to take her pill, so had Chantal. Why did only my reminders work? Was it because she associated me with the pills? Or was this a protest against my having gone away? Was I supposed to feel guilty?

Even after skipping five pills in a row, though, she was better than she had been a month before. That night, when we got off on a conversational tangent, she said, "Now what were we talking about?" The fact that she could follow a conversation well enough to distinguish a tangent signified a world of change.

By the time Wendy came for her weekly visit a few days later, Barb was back on schedule and it showed. She'd dressed carefully, was talkative and witty, more settled and relaxed. After Wendy left, I dug out an old photo album and Barb sat next to me on the couch as I leafed through it. I wanted to get her talking about the family.

She was mostly quiet as she studied vacation photos from trips to Lake Geneva, Wisconsin, but responded to my baby pictures with cries of "Oh, cute!" The album was a chronological jumble, with black-and-white snapshots from the fifties mixed with color shots from the sixties and seventies, so there was no predicting what would appear from one page to the next, no preparing for the shock when I flipped yet another page of old vacation shots and came face-to-face with Barb's wedding pictures.

I braced for her reaction, but the shock was all mine. She didn't seem to remember the event. What interested her most, though distantly, were the guests. She pointed each one out by name, easily pronouncing the Arabic words I hadn't heard in so long, completely skipping over Karim. Even stranger than her non-reaction to the groom was how she ignored the bride. She hardly seemed to recognize the radiant girl at the center of those forty-year-old photos.

We were back on track, and now that Barb was improving she seemed to crave conversation. I worried about her being alone so much and possibly lonely. The caregivers didn't always show up; scheduling was as complicated as ever. I went twice a week, and either Tom or I called almost every day, but I wondered what she did the rest of the time, when the only voices she heard, other than the ones on TV, were the voices in her head.

March 25: Day 25

Sunday. Bad day—nothing like Friday. I go early and bring food. She's mumbling and distracted, doesn't smile, doesn't laugh, not happy to see me. I suggest calling Tom and Sylvia—Sylvia's visiting Tom this weekend—and she says let's put it off. Later I call and we leave a message but she's wooden on the phone. It seems like she's off her meds but when I check, two more are gone since Friday.

It's discouraging. Even more discouraging is the fact that it's a freakishly beautiful day—80 degrees in March, in Chicago—and she won't even go on the porch. I keep asking her to take her pill and she keeps saying she'll do it at bedtime. I say okay but wonder if she'll remember. I have to ask Wendy if there's some way she can be dosed once a week.

One strange thing I started to notice as Barb interacted more was that she knew things she didn't seem to have any way of knowing. Carol, a manager at CMSS, told me when she'd called one day, Barb had asked if she was feeling better. Carol wondered how Barb had known she'd been ill. Another time, I'd arrived late for a meeting with Wendy, and when I got there, Barb commented on the heavy traffic on Oakton Street. She hadn't been out of the house in decades. How did she even remember Oakton Street, let alone know that ten minutes earlier I'd been stuck in traffic there? They were small things and could have been coincidences, but they happened more and more. In particular, she seemed to know what I was thinking. Maybe it was just a highly developed kind of intuition, but I began to wonder if she was selectively psychic and tuned in specifically to me. It didn't seem so far-fetched after everything else that had happened lately.

That day there was yet another incident. I told her I'd read some of the letters she'd written from Iraq. "Why don't you put them in a book?" she said.

"Wow," I said. "You're psychic. I was thinking of doing something like that. Is that okay?"

"Yes," she said, not seeming very interested. She was arranging coconut cookies in a precise pattern on a plate. Since she'd broached the subject, I pressed a little.

"I was thinking of writing a book about you. What do you think about that?"

"Do it," she replied, amiable but still without much interest. "Would you like a cookie?"

I'd been planning to ask her permission, wondering how and when to go about it, and indeed what constituted permission in her case, whether she'd understand the question or the idea of what I was proposing. Now she'd suggested it.

The conversation made me wonder again if she was reading my thoughts. It was disconcerting, but if true, it helped to explain her cooperation. If she knew what I was thinking, she knew the pills were good for her. Or maybe it just meant she trusted me. Whatever was going on, though, one thing was for sure. There was no fooling her.

March 28: Day 28

I call Barb in the morning and she sounds great. I ask Deborah to confirm that she's up to date on her pills and she says yes, there's only two left and tells me the new meds arrived the day before, as planned. At first the pharmacy wanted me to pick them up once a month, but when I explained our situation they agreed to deliver them. Another gift.

Deborah puts Barb on the phone and she sounds good. Happy. Rational. So it's a good day, not just for her but also for me. When she's up and focused it makes my day and when she sounds blank or hostile or, worse, when I can't reach her and I know she's there alone maybe being terrorized by her voices, my day is ruined, especially a dark rainy day like this when I feel I should drop everything and go over there but know that if I do my work day is shot. This is a good day.

Here's how well she's doing. I tell her I'll be over in two days and ask if she wants me to bring anything special when I come. I say it confusingly, though, and she stops me. "Wait, what? Say that again," she says. A month earlier she wouldn't have bothered to try to understand, would have just said good or no. Now her mind is clear enough to call me on it when mine isn't.

· · · ◆ · · ·

Except for briefly at my father's memorial service, I hadn't seen my friend Kim in months. She lived over an hour away and we were both busy. Barb's house, though, was midway—I suggested we meet there for dinner on a Friday night.

March 30: Day 30

Kim arrives while Wendy is there and for a while it's the four of us. As she had when Maria was there, Barb seems to enjoy hanging out in a group of women, talking, laughing. After Wendy leaves we order a pizza and

Barb puts a dance DVD in the player. When the pizza arrives Barb fills her plate and withdraws from the table but eats nearby, instead of at her usual post in the hall. She listens to us talk and joins in sometimes.

She even plays hostess a little, something I see her do with Wendy too. As we get drinks in the kitchen, Barb asks Kim if she wants a cup or a glass for her 7up. Kim says she doesn't mind drinking out of the can. "That's ridiculous," Barb says. "I'll get you a cup."

The most remarkable thing that happened that day had to do with books. Kim had just opened a used bookstore and I'd brought her a stack of paperbacks I'd finished. When I set the books down on the dining room table, Barb drifted over and began browsing. I was a little surprised. She hadn't seemed interested in reading in a long time. I asked her if she wanted to keep any.

"Thank you," she said, scooping up the whole pile and heading for the stairs.

When she came back down, empty-handed, Wendy asked if she liked to read. Her reply seemed to surprise her almost as much as it did the rest of us.

"I hadn't read in years," she said, looking thoughtful. "But lately I've started again."

April

On April 1, Fritz and I took groceries and lunch to Barb and she hung around while we ate, a new thing for her. We watched *Something's Gotta Give*—her choice from a new batch of movies Tom had sent—and though as usual she didn't follow the plot, she liked the music. When the Marvin Gaye song "Let's Get It On" began to play she turned to me and said, "Is that Otis Redding?"

On April 2, one month and one day after she started taking Risperdal, Barb answered the phone. She just picked it up and said hello.

After a short and otherwise inconsequential conversation I emailed my brother to tell him the news and then doubted what I'd heard was real. Maybe I'd imagined it. Maybe I'd misunderstood, maybe Chantal had been there and picked it up and handed it to her. But no, a few days later she did it again when Tom called, without any acknowledgment on her part that it was in any way unusual. She began picking up regularly, though not reliably, and we developed a phone routine. We talked about the weather and what we'd eaten that day. I told her about my doings, she told me what she'd watched on TV. At last I had a way to check on her. At last she was beginning to reconnect with the world outside her own mind.

On April 6, Dr. Weinstein came for a follow-up visit. As before, he was only available Thursday afternoon. I couldn't cancel my class again so Wendy went and reported the next day that everything had gone fine. "Barb was charming as ever," she wrote in an email. She reported that the doctor was so impressed with Barb's improvement that he'd increased the dose, doubled it, in fact, though at 0.5 mg it was still child-size.

On April 8, I went to the house to let the plumber in. Again. He brought an assistant this time and they cleared the line forty feet into the yard and charged accordingly. Later I found a note Barb had written to herself on the back of an envelope: *Ask M about the sink.*

After the plumber left, I got us lunch and sat down at the kitchen table, expecting Barb to carry her plate to the next room, as she always did. Instead, she sat down next to me and started to eat.

I sat perfectly still for a while as everything in my world reorganized itself a little. Finally I dared to reach for my sandwich. I tried to make no sudden moves lest she bolt, like some rare and skittish animal. But she didn't. She got up for ketchup—that's it, I thought, now she's gone—then sat down again. We ate our lunch, talked about the food, and when we'd finished eating, she picked up both plates and took them to the sink. Again, she didn't acknowledge that anything unusual had happened though it had been nearly thirty years since we'd eaten at a table together. Again, I was amazed, and grateful for this small reciprocity. I felt like I'd been calling into outer space and finally, after years, had heard a faint reply.

After lunch, Barb showed me the faded, peeling Parcheesi board on the dining room table, the one I'd given my parents for Christmas thirty years before. She said she'd been playing with Bev, one of the caregivers. She turned the board over and said they'd played the game on the back too. Le Jeu Joli. I asked her what that meant and she said, "The beautiful flower." Then she said, "The beautiful game." Then she said, "The sour clown."

The sour clown!

The next time Fritz and I went for Sunday dinner the three of us played Parcheesi. Barb won.

The next step, I thought, would be getting her to leave the house but that turned out to be more difficult. Whatever fears or beliefs had dissolved enough to make it possible for her to answer the phone and eat at a table with me were less daunting than those that kept her inside. Whenever I suggested going for a walk or a drive she simply and firmly refused. As a first step, Wendy and I schemed how to get her onto the porch.

Barb was as preoccupied as ever with the details of how things looked, constantly adjusting the alignment and placement of objects and furniture, forever brushing lint off my sleeve, dog hair from my skirt. The three folding chairs on the front porch bothered her. She wanted them moved out of sight. One day when Wendy was there she complained again about the chairs—she wanted them folded and leaned against the far wall. So Wendy and I went out to put them away and invited her to join us. We stood in the middle of the porch while Barb hung back, in the doorway. "Come on," we said. "We'll each fold one."

I volunteered to go first. I strode to the back of the porch, picked up a chair, folded it with a flourish, and leaned it against the wall. I took a bow. Barb and Wendy applauded. Next Wendy took her turn. Then, like swimmers who'd successfully dived from a tall cliff and were treading water below, waiting for the last and most timid diver to join them, we stood at the far end of the porch beckoning Barb to take her turn and fold the last chair.

She stood in the doorway, pale and tense, and then, with a determined look, darted toward us. She got halfway across the porch before she froze. Wendy and I cheered her on but she shook her head and rushed back into the house. She couldn't do it. Her fears, her demons, her delusions, her menacing voices, whatever was holding her back wouldn't let her go and I felt a little sorry for having tried to make her. At moments like this she reminded me so much of my mother who, though terrified, had once allowed me to coax her onto an escalator.

A couple weeks later, Barb asked me to throw away the packaging from the TV that was still piled on the front porch. When Fritz had unpacked it, he'd folded the box neatly and left it there, out of sight in consideration for Barb, but within reach in case we needed it later. I'd forgotten it was there; Barb obviously hadn't.

I grabbed as much of the packaging as I could but the tidy arrangement Fritz had left fell apart when I lifted it. Plastic wrap and a profusion of packing peanuts spilled all over the porch. I dragged what I could to the garbage can in the back alley, leaving the mess on the porch for a second trip.

The day was unseasonably warm and neighbors were outside, working in their yards. As I wrestled the cardboard into the garbage some old friends of my father's appeared for a visit. We talked for a while and then I went back to finish cleaning up.

The mess on the porch was gone. Every little Styrofoam peanut, every scrap of plastic that I'd dropped had been picked up, carried away and stuffed into the kitchen wastebasket. Barb, showing no sign of recent exertion, let alone terror at having ventured onto the porch, was back in her chair, placidly watching TV. Apparently obsessive compulsive disorder trumped agoraphobia. My sister had overcome her fear of leaving the house to clean up after me, her perpetually messy little sister.

Pretty soon other long-dormant parts of Barb's personality began to reassert themselves. One day in mid-April I drove to the house with two fruit smoothies—I was on a campaign to get Barb to eat something other than potato chips and cookies—and when I arrived she told me she'd started "annotating books." She showed me a Jehovah's Witness tract left by one of the caregivers in which she'd underlined passages and written skeptical notes in the margins.

"Propaganda!" she'd written on one page. Elsewhere, next to a passage about death, she'd written, in capital letters, *"How do you know?"* Then she showed me my father's copy of Garrison Keillor's *The Book of Guys.* She'd written *"old dudes"* in the margin and underlined the sentence "Go ahead and fart" with a special wavy line.

On April 28, Maria came for a second visit. Most of her work was in homeless shelters. She knew how to talk to Barb without insulting or scaring her.

Maria: Do you ever have any pain?

Barb: Yes, sometimes.

Maria: Where?

Barb (looking down): I'm not going to tell you.

Maria, cheerily: Well, I respect your privacy, but if you ever want help with it, I may be able to do something so let me know.

Another discovery that week—in addition to the troubling fact that Barb had pain she wouldn't discuss—was that she'd started to keep a notebook. I was still trying to count her pills, which she moved around the house from day to day, and found it when I was looking for her stash. For years she'd kept a stack of notebooks on her desk, and occasionally I flipped one open, but they'd always been blank. Now, in the same shaky round handwriting in which she composed her grocery lists, she'd filled pages with weirdly thoughtful insights, lists of slant rhymes and comments in quasi-medical language that seemed inspired by my father's illness.

Some of the writing looked like poetry, some like a diary. There was a short list:

People who died:
1. Hawkins
2. The Hajji
3. Grandma Hawkins

Other pages looked like research notes, though on what, I couldn't tell. There were references to Hamas fighters, psychogenetics, Chief Illiniwek, gas attacks and—to my surprise—various childhood crushes of mine I hadn't thought about in forty years. Sometimes she recorded observations—*"Everything is educational"*—and sometimes she seemed to be writing about one of us, most often my father— *"He used a magno to defrost a turkey."* Her writing had all the qualities I told my students to cultivate—original language, striking imagery, personal truth—I just didn't know what any of it meant.

May

Not long after we met, Wendy asked if I'd speak to Wilpower's monthly family support group so one unseasonably warm Monday night in May I showed up and tried to tell our story. It was hot, I was nervous. But I wanted to get the word out, tell anyone who would listen that I had proof that change was possible.

Afterward there were a lot of questions. How did I plan to proceed in the future? What about raising the dose? How could they get someone on SSI? Some kind person even offered to visit Barb. Then Sharon raised her hand. I'd seen her before at meetings. She was about my age, maybe younger. She looked tired. I knew she had a schizophrenic daughter.

"How do you feel about having to do all this?" she asked. "Aren't you a little pissed off? Don't you resent it? I would."

I hadn't expected questions about my mental state. "Oh no," I said. "Really not. I welcome the opportunity to help. It feels good to finally be able to do something."

My little speech effectively silenced Sharon, as it was meant to. And it was true, at least partly. Even largely. But I could tell by Sharon's skeptical smirk that she didn't buy it, and for months afterward her face would drift into my mind when I was lying in bed unable to sleep, trying to add up columns of numbers. It took me months to figure out why, to realize I'd missed yet another opportunity for honest discussion. I was doing what my family had always done, keeping secrets from myself.

····◆····

Money was a constant worry. The day after my talk at Wilpower I went to the house to let the plumber in, this time to fix the upstairs sink. Then I drove across town to meet with an accountant about my father's taxes—apparently we owed even more than we'd thought. I'd just written a check for real estate taxes, another one to the cemetery. Every month I got a bill for caregivers.

I lay awake every night crunching numbers. Caregivers were still the biggest expense. Barb no longer seemed to need four-hour visits, but since it wasn't worth it to them to come for just an hour we were still paying for daily four-hour shifts. I'd asked Wendy early on if there might be some way caregiving was included in Barb's benefits, but after asking around, she said no. I waited a few months as expenses piled up and then asked again. I didn't want to press my luck—so much help had already come our way.

This time Wendy contacted our old ally, the North Shore Senior Center, and on May 16 she emailed me with incredible news. Because Barb was over sixty-two, and couldn't live independently without help, she qualified for free daily home services through the Illinois Department on Aging. This changed everything. I'd need to fill out forms and meet with social workers to prove that Barb qualified, but help was in sight. For the first time since this had all begun I began to think that not only Barb could get her life back but that maybe I could too.

June

Not only was Barb's will coming back, so was her sense of humor.

Tom and I had begun to plan for the burial of my father's ashes, which had sat in a ceramic urn on the buffet since December. As the date for the burial approached, I mentioned the plan to Barb one Friday when Wendy and Maria were there and asked if she wanted to attend the burial. "No," she said flatly, hefting the urn I'd handed her. "I'll hold down the fort."

Maria had spent her last few visits trying to talk Barb into agreeing to let a mobile medical team come over to give her a more thorough physical exam, including a blood test. Barb always demurred, and this day, although she'd allowed Maria to take her blood pressure again, she was firmer than ever about not wanting to see a doctor. Maria thought it was important and kept pressing.

Maria: What do you think, Barb? Can't they just come over and give you a checkup?

Barb, gesturing toward the urn: They can come over and see which one of us is dead.

··· ◆ ···

I spent the morning of June 5, what would have been my father's ninetieth birthday, at the cemetery, trying to straighten out the plan for the burial. They'd lost the record of our previous meeting, wouldn't confirm anything by phone, and wanted more money. I drove from there to meet the Illinois Department on Aging social worker at the house. On the way, I stopped to pick up lunch for Barb in what I figured was a fitting if on-the-fly birthday tribute to my frugal father—hot dogs from Superdawg.

The real tribute to his frugality, though, turned out to be the meeting, which didn't take long. After a brief interview with Barb, and a glance at her birth certificate to confirm her age, the social worker authorized full benefits. We qualified for up to twenty hours a week of home visits—nineteen after I opted to spend one hour's worth on a Lifeline medical alert device that would connect Barb to a 24-hour emergency system. This meant I could arrange for shorter visits six days a week. Barb would have someone to check on her every day, if I went Sundays, and she'd only be alone one day a week when I was out of town. This meant we could afford to keep her in the house.

I knew it would take awhile for the paperwork to go through and then more time to find the right person, but when we did, the visits would be covered, free. This changed everything.

· · · ◆ · · ·

Friday, June 8 was a beautiful day and another first. Despite that summer's buzzing, swarming plague of 17-year cicadas, Barb agreed to sit on the screened back porch. When Wendy arrived she joined us, knowing what an important occasion the first porch visit was. Barb was in high spirits, blithely indifferent to the occasional renegade bug that made it through the ripped screens. Once again, she showed no sign that a shift had taken place. She served us drinks and snacks, commented on the beautiful weather, told us she'd finished reading *Oedipus Rex* and said she'd started *Macbeth*. Only when a cicada thudded blindly into Wendy did we all decide to go inside.

When I got to the house the following Sunday, Barb was in particularly good form. Alice, one of the caregivers Barb liked, had been there two days running and had brought a DVD of *The Ten Commandments* for them to watch together. I said I thought Alice sounded nice. Barb said, "Yes, she is nice. She wears orange shorts."

I'd brought groceries, lunch, three new porch chairs. I swept up the dead cicadas, set up the chairs, found a folding table in the pantry and set that up. The back porch was a nice place to sit if you didn't mind flaking paint, broken screens or the fact that the floor had an approximately nineteen-degree slope earthward. We ate lunch there, waving to incredulous neighbors who passed, and afterward stayed to read the newspaper as if we did it every Sunday.

I'd gone shopping the week before and bought Barb some summer clothes—a pair of cropped linen pants like a pair of mine she'd admired and some khaki cargo shorts. Tom had sent T-shirts. She tried it all on and everything fit. She was set for summer.

I hoped the things I was spending money on were life-enhancing—porch chairs, summer clothes, food—and wondered if it was okay to buy her linen pants, even if they were from Costco, while accepting Department on Aging benefits. I hoped so. I hoped the money would get easier. I couldn't wait to stop worrying.

· · · ◆ · · ·

The next Friday I took Max when I went to visit. It was risky. Barb had been afraid of him since that first failed meeting ten years earlier. Whenever I'd brought him to see my father, she'd withdrawn into her room with one of my grandfather's antique canes for protection and slammed the door. I didn't want to invade what was now her space with something unnecessarily scary. Nurses and psychiatrists were one thing, her part of the deal to make it possible for her to stay there. Dogs were another. But I still had my pet therapy fantasy, and Max loved car rides, especially now that it was top-down season. Besides, Wendy wanted to meet him.

I needn't have worried, though. Now that Barb was getting better, Max was another nonissue. She patted him on the head, called him dear, and fed him grapes. From then on they were friends.

The following Sunday, we watched DVDs from a new batch Tom had sent. First we watched *The Adventures of Milo and Otis*, a sentimental animal story with a musical background. Barb kept commenting on the score—"Isn't that a Chopin etude?" Then we watched *Clueless*, which she pronounced "Cute!" She sat next to me on the couch the whole time. I thought again of how she reminded me of my cat, companionable but ready to spring away at a moment's notice for reasons I couldn't begin to guess.

July

When it became clear that Barb was reading again, I asked if she wanted me to bring her more books, and if so, what titles. She requested a booklist, so I printed out the Modern Library's list of the hundred best English language novels, and Barb picked *A Passage to India* and *To the Lighthouse*. The next time I visited, I brought both.

A week later, when she told me she was reading *A Passage to India*, I asked her what it was about. "Some ladies hanging out at a club," she said. *To the Lighthouse*, she said, was "by some old bag that killed herself."

I felt stung. She'd called Virginia Woolf an old bag. I supposed she'd picked up *old bag* from my father but still, it was a painful, dated, sexist term, particularly since, at sixty-three, she qualified as one herself. She didn't see herself that way, though, didn't seem to think of herself as having aged at all, despite the fact that it was her very age that made us eligible for benefits that would allow her to continue to live the way she wanted.

The Illinois Department on Aging had hooked us up with another agency that was now bringing food every Friday morning. Barb seemed to enjoy the sociability as much as the food. She liked answering the door to the friendly delivery ladies—"nice old bags"— who also brought in her mail and the newspaper. She liked to stow the groceries, stacking the little frozen dinners neatly in the freezer, tucking the fruit into a neat row in the produce drawer below, lining the juice boxes up precisely on the refrigerator shelf.

The first week they'd come, Barb showed me all the food she'd put away and offered me a child-sized carton of *haleeb*.

"What's that?" I said.

She shrugged, a little disappointed in me for not knowing. "Arabic for milk."

···◆···

We'd been authorized for benefits for a month but still hadn't found a caregiver who could come when we needed her. Then they put me in touch with Yvonne Flowers and on Monday, July 16, she came to the house. She was my age. She was smart and kind and businesslike. Later I would learn she was also practical, trustworthy, conscientious, consistent, compassionate. She had a sense of humor. She even knew how to fix a toilet. And she was settled. She wasn't going to disappear on a whim. To my enormous relief, she agreed to start right away.

On Thursday, July 26, Tom flew in for the Friday morning burial of my father's ashes. I picked him up at the airport and drove him to Superdawg, then back to the house. We'd been in touch almost daily but this would be the first time he'd seen Barb since December. I wanted him to be impressed with how improved she was.

If I'd hoped for some kind of dramatic reunion, though, it didn't happen. The house was hot, my anxiety was palpable, and Barb was petulant. The visit was tense. I'd expected too much.

The next morning Tom, Fritz, and I buried my father's ashes in a simple ceremony we'd made up the night before. Afterward, we went to lunch at Hackney's, my father's favorite outdoor restaurant, then back to the house with carryout food for Barb. We were still elated from having improvised a last bit of theater on my father's behalf and tried to describe to Barb the hovering, solicitous cemetery personnel, the poems we'd read, the graveside martinis Fritz had mixed and passed around, which we'd then poured into the open grave. Barb listened humorlessly and, when we were done, informed me that the toilet was acting up again.

Tom and I got up early the next day to be back at the house for our seven-thirty emergency appointment with the plumber, and while we waited for him to show up, the three of us sat down at the kitchen table for breakfast. It was a practical visit, not a social or therapeutic one, and I had no expectations. It was too early in the morning for that. But maybe because nobody was trying to make it into anything special, it was. Here was our reunion, over Egg McMuffins and weak carryout coffee. The last time we'd had breakfast together at this table, I thought, we'd all been young and optimistic, at least about each other's futures. We never could have predicted this particular moment. It was a bittersweet thought until I remembered that only six months earlier we couldn't have predicted it either, couldn't have imagined that things would turn out this well.

···◆···

Trying to describe conversations with my sister is impossible. I write down the words, but I can't evoke the meaning. Something passes between us when we speak that makes more sense than the words themselves but it's a meaning that's hard to hold on to.

I found a piece of torn cardboard in my car on which I'd written notes from a conversation we had one fairly typical July day. First there's a short grocery list of unremarkable things my sister wants in the middle of a heat wave—ice, root beer, popsicles. Below that there's this:

Barb: I've started remembering things.

Me: Good.

Barb: Do you hear them talking at night?

Me: Do you?

Barb: Sometimes. It's good. Sometimes it's too quiet. Too quiet isn't good.

Barb, later: I keep worrying about Christmas.

This last bit I would have remembered even if I hadn't written it down. She looked so anxious when she said it. It reminded me so much of my mother, her melancholy around the holidays.

Around that time I heard a program on NPR about siblings of schizophrenics. I was in my car, driving into the city on a Saturday morning to make the rounds of the galleries, looking for something to write about for my weekly column, and almost ran off the road when I heard the brother of a schizophrenic describe us as "frozen souls."

"We're always waiting to start our lives," he said. "But we can't. We feel too guilty."

Then they aired a segment about Pamela Spiro Wagner and Dr. Carolyn S. Spiro, identical twin sisters who'd written a book together called *Divided Minds*. One was a psychiatrist, the other a poet. The poet was schizophrenic. The segment ended with a conversation between the sisters about whether drinking out of a chipped teacup hurts the feelings of the teacup. The schizophrenic sister thinks that it might; the other sister tries to explain why it doesn't. It's weird and funny and sweet, to me at least. It reminds me of my conversations with Barb. We talk about whether the TV wants me more than it wants her. She says it does. I insist that it doesn't.

A few weeks later, I remember this conversation on a Sunday morning when I bring Barb groceries, a newspaper, and a pumpkin. The pumpkin was her request—she showed me a picture of one as if without reference I might not know what to buy. It's eighty degrees and we sit together on the back porch while we read the newspaper, by now an ordinary event that still feels extraordinary to me. Barb puts out bowls of potato chips and pretzels and pours us Cokes. We sit in the sun and she passes me the parts of the newspaper she's finished.

She always starts with travel and then reads the news. After a while she looks up with a worried expression.

"A ship killed a blue whale," she says.

"Oh, that's sad," I say.

She looks sideways, like a cartoon character having a second thought, and says, "Or a blue whale killed a ship."

"Hmm," I say.

"Or maybe they killed each other," she continues, still looking away. She seems to be listening for something, maybe for a transmission at a frequency too high for me to hear, and then, apparently getting her answer, turns back to me, nodding and smiling knowingly, and says, "They collapsed together."

When she talks like this, these little riffs she does sound like jokes or poems or dreams, but I think she means them to be true. And, here's the strange thing—they seem true to me too.

August

Yvonne being there made everything better. Barb and Yvonne got along right away. Barb made out grocery lists and Yvonne went shopping. Yvonne made popcorn and they watched movies together. They discussed the newspaper. Yvonne talked Barb into letting her wash her clothes in the washing machine instead of scrubbing them by hand in the small upstairs sink. Yvonne was the one to call my attention to the broken bedsprings in Barb's mattress, sharp points of metal that had torn through the fabric cover and gouged Barb's legs.

It seemed like horrible negligence. Who knew how long she'd been sleeping on something like a bed of nails. At the very least, it was a symptom of how uncommunicative we'd all been. Barb had never complained, and no one noticed because she made her own bed—with military precision and artful combinations of sheets and pillowcases—until one day Yvonne changed the sheets and saw metal spikes sticking out of the mattress. The next Sunday Fritz and I went to the local Bedding Experts and bought Barb a new Serta. Within an hour it was on her bed and the old mattress was in the alley.

One afternoon Barb told me she and Yvonne had seen Elvis.

"Really?" I said.

"Yes," she said. "And he was *very good*."

Of course. It was August 19, 2007. Three days earlier had been the thirtieth anniversary of Elvis's death. Feeling a little like the mean kid who breaks the news that there's no Santa, I tried to explain. Elvis had died, I said, leaving out the thirty-years-ago part. Maybe they'd watched a tribute concert?

It was her turn to say "Really?" in a tone that said she wasn't sure she believed it. I didn't press. Why impose my reality on her when hers was better?

September

On Sundays we read the newspaper together. We read each other amusing stories. I specialized in arts and human interest. She preferred travel, crime, and international terror. We showed each other cute pictures of animals. One day she started to read me a story about a man who'd been arrested for driving nude on the Indiana Tollway. She looked up midway through to gauge my attention and then, seeing she'd gotten it, read the ending with perfect comic timing: "He says he's more comfortable that way."

On a warm Sunday afternoon in mid-September I attended the opening of a show I'd curated at the Evanston Art Center. It was a happy event, a good show, beautifully installed, well attended by satisfied artists. Afterward I felt a rush of relief and loneliness. I wanted to celebrate. I headed for Barb's house, stopping at a Chinese restaurant on the way because Yvonne had told me Barb likes Chinese food. I was hungry and couldn't decide what to get and ended up buying enough food for a party of six—fried rice, beef and broccoli, oyster sauce, egg foo young, sweet and sour pork, wonton soup, egg rolls.

I'd brought her groceries too, which I'd stashed in the car on my way to the opening, and I showed up at the house with over a hundred dollars' worth of food. For my tiny sister. It was ridiculous and I thought of how my father would cringe and carp at these excesses but I enjoyed Barb's delight as she unpacked it all. I didn't have time for thrift. Thrift takes planning and presence of mind. Mostly I was just winging it.

I also brought her a white blouse I'd bought years before for myself that never quite fit and which I'd never worn but never been able to part with. Just that week, I'd realized it was perfect for Barb. So I arrived with all this bounty and it took me four trips to get it into the house. I laid all the stuff on the kitchen table and she loved the blouse, loved the Chinese food, loved the head of iceberg lettuce, the two tomatoes, the pound cake. She put everything away and then served us dinner and afterward divided the remaining food into two equal portions and gave me one neatly wrapped package to take home.

She seemed to sense that I was the one who needed to be taken care of that day and suggested we watch a movie. Tom had sent a DVD of *The Terminal*. "Okay," I said. Why not? I'd done my work for the day. I had nowhere else to be.

We put the movie in. I tried to get her to do it, but she couldn't get the movie to play and finally gave up and handed the remote to me saying, "It wants you." We sat side by side on the couch and watched, but the day was taking its toll and I began to slip into a reclining position. She got up.

"Don't go," I said, retracting my feet.

"No," she said. "You need your legroom. Can I get you a blanket?"

She'd moved to a nearby chair and seemed comfortable enough so I said all right and slid further into the couch. She disappeared upstairs for a minute and returned with an enormous brown blanket— the house was full of things I never knew were there—and spread it over me, tucking it in all around me as I dozed off.

"There," she said, patting my head gently. I fell asleep.

October

Early in October an old friend called to say he was in town. I invited him for dinner and over pasta I told him about Barb. She was all I could think of to talk about anymore, and pretty soon he started talking about his sister with bipolar disorder—her bouts with mania, her wild spending, her arrests, marriages, institutionalizations.

We'd known each other for years, but it was the first I'd heard of any of it. And it wasn't even the first conversation I'd had that week with someone I'd known for years who turned out to have a mentally ill family member. It was a reprise of my experience at the medical library. The more open I was about Barb, the more common I learned it was. My friend's sister was even taking the same medication as Barb. Or rather, she wasn't taking it, a complication that made our situation seem fortunate by comparison.

Barb was taking her pills more or less regularly by then, especially after I stopped nagging her, and I seldom heard her talking to herself. Even when I did hear her, the tone was different, less intense, more subdued, friendly even. Whatever the voices were saying these days was less terrible. She seemed—I was afraid to use the word but it was true—happy.

The next time I was at the house, the phone rang. It was Fritz. We still kept it set on speakerphone, so I heard both sides of the conversation.

Barb: Hello?

Fritz: Hi, Barb, it's Fritz! How are you?

Barb: Oh, I'm fine. Max is here watching war movies with me.

Fritz: (silence)

What could he say—it sounded delusional but in fact it was exactly true. I'd brought Max, and he was lounging that very minute on the floor in front of the TV where he'd been keeping Barb company all afternoon while she watched Ken Burns's World War II documentary on PBS.

The next Sunday I brought Barb lunch and *The New York Times*. As always, she started with the travel section. She read me an article about France, and we swapped stories about our own travels there. Then she said, "The first time I was in Paris some German guy came up behind me in a bar and said, 'Go home. Go back to Chicago.'"

"Really?" I said, putting down my chicken salad sandwich.

She nodded. "I think it had something to do with the mother."

"So," I said, trying not to scare her with my sudden intensity, "did you see this guy? Or did you just hear his voice?"

She looked up, very focused and connected now, like I'd brought up something she'd wanted to talk about, and with a kind of now-that-you-mention-it air she said, "I just heard his voice."

So there it was. She was hearing voices even then, years before anyone thought she was sick, years before she'd ever set foot in Iraq. I remember when she took that trip. She was twenty-one.

She must have wondered then what it meant, to be hearing voices telling her to go home when everyone else she knew was launching themselves into the world. Or maybe she did know and was trying very hard to hide it—from us, from her friends and her teachers, later from her bosses and colleagues, from Karim. No wonder she was so good at being secretive. She'd been living with this even longer than we had.

October 19
Barb, nodding approvingly while watching a girl power cartoon: I think they've cut back a lot on the male chauv thing.

I'm realizing that, however fragile she seems to me, Barb is strong in many ways and thinks of herself as a strong woman. One day Wendy was telling us about her particularly bad week—her dog had been attacked, her car had been broken into—and Barb's response was to console her as if Wendy had become the sick person in the room for a few minutes.

··· ◆ ···

On October 28, we celebrated Barb's sixty-fourth birthday. We discussed it a few days in advance and she suggested we come over on Sunday, my usual day to visit and one day before her actual birthday. I'd wondered how to handle the subject of age, if it came up, since she didn't seem to see herself as having gotten older. But she addressed it herself. "I'm fifty-one years old," she announced, reading my mind as usual.

"Really?" I said. "What year were you born?"

"1920," she said. And then with great seriousness added, "but sometimes I'm one hundred years old." Then she said she wanted a yellow cake with chocolate frosting and vanilla ice cream.

Fritz bought the cake, I bought presents, and we went over on Sunday with food. We lit candles, sang "Happy Birthday." She opened the presents and especially liked the terry cloth dishtowels— "Expensive!"—the pink bed sheets, and the nail file, all items I'd found on lists she'd made and kept hidden around the house. We don't discuss the lists, but she expects me to find them. It's how she lets me know what she wants.

·· · ◆ · ··

Ways in Which Barb Is Like Newman, My Cat
Fastidious
Secretive
With just a little help can get by very well on her own
Sometimes walks away in the middle of things
Good at grooming
Sleeps a lot
Is good at getting me to do things for her
Intelligent
Quiet
Small
Surprising
A little snobbish
Psychic
Eats a lot and never gets fat
Stares at people
Won't get in the car
Allows affection from a select few
You never know exactly what she's thinking
I worry about her on Halloween—people have funny ideas about who it's all right to hurt

November

Thanksgiving. The day marked the one-year anniversary of the beginning of the countdown to my father's death and I dreaded the forced march through the next five weeks of mandatory cheerfulness even more than usual. From now until Christmas every day would remind me of what had happened that day the year before. A year ago at noon, my father couldn't eat. A year ago at eight p.m., he'd been taken to the hospital by ambulance for the last time.

But we were determined to celebrate. I made cranberry sauce. Fritz smoked a turkey. We made pies. And on Thanksgiving Day, we loaded the smoked turkey, the pies, and the cranberry sauce plus the makings for everything else—mashed potatoes, sweet potatoes, brussels sprouts, gravy, appetizers—into the car, along with a few of bottles of wine, three DVDs, Max, and a pile of firewood, and took it all to Barb.

From the beginning the party was more earnest than fun. To help it along, we opened a bottle of wine as soon as we arrived. Barb joined us in a toast but after that withdrew to watch TV and stay out of our way while we cooked. Without my father's stories and speeches, his rhapsodic appreciations of the food and his exhortations about every detail of its handling, the preparations for dinner were a very quiet affair.

Barb was especially subdued, but we were all glum—things weren't going as planned. I'd imagined this would be festive, that she'd hang out in the kitchen, help us cook or at least watch and sip wine along with us. But she sat in front the TV, even more disconnected than usual, and later retreated upstairs to consult furtively with her voices before dinner, something I hadn't seen her do in months. By the time we finally sat down to eat—at least she ate at the table with us—she'd gone from glum to grim.

After dinner my childhood friend Sandy, in town for the holiday, stopped by for a visit. She hadn't seen Barb in years and remarked on how improved she seemed. I was relieved to hear her say so but to me she seemed way off, seemed to have slid back into her fog. "Oh, no," Sandy said, "she's clearly a different person than she was the last time I saw her." Then she said exactly what Deb had said the last time she'd seen my sister: "She reminds me so much of your mother."

It wasn't until I got home that the impact of what my two oldest friends had said hit me. Of course. My sister *was* like my mother. It explained the day's dark mood. My mother was at her saddest on holidays. I needed to remind myself that now that Barb was coming back to herself, she had moods too, like anyone else. Now that her personality had resurfaced, so had her capacity for sadness.

I tried calling the next morning but she didn't pick up. Yvonne was out for the week, and her agency hadn't sent anyone to take her place. I had plans for the day; unless I canceled them, Barb was going to be alone. I wouldn't have worried except she'd acted so strange the day before.

I began an email to my brother describing our subdued Thanksgiving and voicing my worries, but before I finished, I saw the bouncing icon at the bottom of my screen, signaling an incoming email from him. He'd just talked with Barb, he said. She was "in absolutely rare form." She'd described the meal we'd cooked, dish by dish, and told him, with witty asides, about watching *Sicko*—her choice of the movies we'd brought. He concluded she sounded better than ever.

Of course I was relieved. But more than that, I was amazed. How exactly like my mother this was, to suffer through a holiday in grim silence and then, when whatever terrible thing she'd dreaded had not come to pass, to remember it brightly afterward.

····◆····

The Sunday after Thanksgiving, I carried two big boxes of Christmas ornaments up from the basement along with my father's little artificial tree. We'd agreed to decorate for Christmas so that when Tom and Sylvia arrived, the house would be festive. Barb wanted to wait to put the tree up so we stashed most of the stuff in the pantry, but I left the box that held the oldest ornaments on the kitchen table, thinking maybe I'd take one or two home for my own tree as a memento of my childhood Christmases.

We started to dig through the box. Barb was at least as interested in the ancient stuff as I was. I realized I couldn't take just one or two ornaments home. They belonged together, there, in this house. Outside of it, any single one would have just seemed odd and shabby, but there, all together, they possessed a certain residual magic. We held them up one by one, calling out "Remember this? Remember this?" She liked the ones shaped like animals—lambs, cats, bears. I liked the oddities my father made or encouraged us to make—the little balls of wrapping paper stuffed with Kleenex, the steak bone someone painted blue that we hung on the tree every year, the gourd suspended from thread. At the bottom of the box was a little green felt stocking I'd made for my hamster when I was nine.

I held it up for Barb to see. "Look," I said. "Remember this? I made it for Junior."

She glanced over and nodded. "And why not?" she said.

When I left, she was still rummaging purposefully through the old ornaments. Maybe, I thought again, the reason she seems so happy is that it's the first time she's lived on her own.

December

On December 19 I woke up wondering how to commemorate the day. It was the one-year anniversary of my father's death. All I could think of was to go see Barb.

When I arrived, the house smelled like someone had been cooking. I had a fleeting thought of some ghostly presence, my father's spirit returning to make one last pot roast, or just conjure up the whiff of one, but Barb told me she'd had toast with jam for lunch. I picked the mail up from the porch, and while she sorted it, I made us tea. I was stalling. This memorial was going to have to be improvised.

"Barb," I said, "do you realize it's exactly one year ago today that Dad died?"

"Yes, I do," she said, nodding. "It was right before Christmas."

"Right!" I said, encouraged. "Things are different now, aren't they, with Dad gone?" I didn't know where to go with this. I wanted to see what she'd say.

"People get cranky when they get old," is what she said.

"That's true," I said.

"He was mad about everything."

"What was he so mad about?"

"He was mad it got cold," she said, implying a rhyme. *He was mad he got old.* It was a poetic leap I wouldn't put past her.

She also seemed mad, upset that I'd brought up this subject. She was slamming things around the kitchen now, and it was the closest we'd come to an argument since all this started. She changed the subject to the broken toilet—now the handle didn't work—and asked me to fix it. She knew the fastest way to deflate me was to start complaining about the plumbing. Then she went back to her newspaper and I returned to the kitchen and my tea.

After a few minutes she hurried in.

"Look, it's Elvis!" She showed me the photo of an Elvis impersonator in the newspaper.

"Didn't you see Elvis?" I asked.

"Yes. Yvonne and I saw him on TV," she said. Then she looked sideways and said, "But she told me he died."

I wasn't sure if the *she* she was referring to was one of her voices or Yvonne or if she'd started talking about me in the third person, maybe as a punishment for having mentioned my father.

"Yes, he died," I said, still feeling guilty for having been the one to tell her, for being the great deflater, the announcer of all deaths. "But did you know that people came from all over the world for his funeral?"

She nodded solemnly. "He was a folk hero and a priest."

A little later, I tried to bring up the subject of change again, this time without mentioning my father. It was the end of the semester and I'd been working on grades so I framed it that way.

"Barb? How would you grade your life now?"

"Oh, it's all right. It's okay. Up and down."

"Do you mean you have mood swings?"

"Yes. People do."

"Do you like living alone?"

"Yvonne comes every day."

"What would make your life better?"

She thought it over, then said, "Oh, maybe more family in a better mood."

Taken aback, defensive now, I tried to figure out what she meant by that. Maybe she was talking about the past, as if I'd asked what *would have made* her life better. Or at least, I hoped so. I hoped she wasn't complaining about me, turning the subject of mood swings back on me, though come to think of it, she might have been. She was right, though, about the past, if that's what she meant. More family in a better mood would have made things better.

But I was frustrated. I was talking about the present and I wanted her to say how splendidly improved her life was and she wasn't cooperating.

She went back into the living room and seated herself in front of the little Christmas tree, which she and Yvonne had carefully loaded with every ornament they could fit and under which they had spread a red felt tree skirt. I turned my attention back to the bills. We stayed that way for a while, not speaking, until she rushed into the kitchen again with her newspaper, all smiles and eye contact this time, and started to read to me. "A woman sat on Santa Claus's lap at a mall in Connecticut," she said, looking up to make sure I was listening. I nodded, smiled. I expected something sappy and sweet, but then she broke into her broadest, most charming smile and said, "And now Santa is suing her for sexual harassment! *Isn't that cute?*"

· · · ◆ · · ·

So here we are. Barb has her sense of humor back. She knows that Elvis is dead. She knows Dad is gone and is willing to reconcile with him at least to the point where she can write off his behavior, some of it at least, to the crankiness of old age. She can make her own meals and make up her own version of the truth. That's already a lot.

And she can live alone in this creaky old house with a little help from a lot of people—from Yvonne, Wendy, Maria, me, Fritz, Tom, the women who deliver the Friday food boxes, the pharmacy that delivers the meds, the anonymous neighbors who shovel the walk and toss the newspaper onto the porch. Thank you, whoever you are. She doesn't complain much, but there are limits to her good nature and she won't let me talk her into a Pollyanna version of her life—a life which, she reports, is up and down.

So here we are after all this time, not in paradise exactly, but far better off than anyone thought possible. Sometimes I wonder whom Barb would have turned out to be if she hadn't gotten sick, and for a while I was even hoping she could still become that person. Sometimes I miss that person. Sometimes I miss the person I would have been if none of this had happened, and I miss the sister I was planning to finally catch up with and become friends with. But she doesn't exist. This person here now is who my sister is, and the sickness as well as the braininess and the humor and the sweetness and the weirdness and the bravery and the charm and the occasional imperious crankiness are all part of that. Up and down, as she said.

At least she gets to have that. Up as well as down. And whose life isn't up and down, I thought, as I said goodbye in the bleak winter light and made my way down the sagging, icy back stairs—next time I'd have to remember to salt them—out through the snow to my salt-encrusted car and home through the dirty slush and the rush-hour traffic to a pile of papers to grade and bills to pay and the uncertain future that awaited me.

As I drove I kept thinking of Barb, sitting in front of the little Christmas tree she and Yvonne had decorated so carefully without any help or advice from me. I'd offered, when I put it up, but she'd demurred. Maybe she and Yvonne would do it later, she'd said. Now

I realized, with a tiny complicated chime of belated recognition, what she'd meant. She'd had plans! She and Yvonne had made plans that didn't include me. Without my even noticing, what I'd wished for had happened. Barb had her life back.

Reading Group Discussion Guide

We hope these questions will stimulate discussion of the many complex issues raised in this book. They can be taken in order or chosen at random. It's up to you and what works best for your discussion and/or group. Thank you for reading and talking and giving thought to how mental illness and treatment are affected by family secrecy.

- Have you ever known someone like Barb, who seemed to have unlimited promise and then became severely mentally ill? How did that affect his or her family?

- Barb spent three years in Iraq and came home very ill. Do you think her living there played a part in the onset of her illness or was the timing coincidental?

- Do you think Barb's parents did the right thing by refusing to hospitalize her when she first came home?

- Some people believe that everyone contains aspects of every mental illness and that severely ill people just have them in greater degrees. Do you agree?

- Do you know someone who has ever heard voices? Have you? Does hearing voices always mean a person is schizophrenic or can there be other explanations?

- If someone you loved and felt responsible for – a parent, a child, a sibling, a spouse, a friend – had a mental breakdown would you know what to do? What would it be?

- How understanding are your family members, friends and colleagues about mental illness?

- How comfortable would you be addressing a cruel joke told by someone else about mental illness, rather than just passing it off?

- Can you accept mental illness as an individual trait like other human differences?

- Often mental illness seems to coincide with high intelligence, artistic talent or strong religious conviction. Are these symptoms of the disease or factors that make people more susceptible to it? Or is this an illusion because mentally ill people who have these qualities are more expressive of them?

- What is the difference between religious mysticism and mental illness?

- Margaret notices that Barb often seems to read her mind and wonders if Barb has psychic powers related to her illness. Other authors writing about schizophrenia, such as Mark Vonnegut and Patrick Tracey, have suggested this possibility as well. What do you think and what does this suggest about the human mind?

- Barb's family suffered from multi-generational mental illness, but Barb was the only one of three children, to become severely ill. Do you think this is just odds or were there other factors that made her vulnerable?

- Should people with a family history of mental illness raise children differently than other people? Should they even have children?

- When Barb begins to take medication Margaret allows Barb to think the pills are a kind of vitamin and wonders if it's right to persuade her to take pills she may not fully understand the nature of. What do you think about that?

- If someone is mentally ill and is not able to take care of him or herself, to what extent should that person's wishes be honored when it comes to making decisions about her care? What if she says she *wants* to sleep in the park?

- Do you think a normal, relatively healthy person can have a primary relationship with a mentally ill person – marriage, close friendship, reciprocal sibling relationship – or should the healthy person let that relationship go and move on?

- What was the turning point that made Barb start to get better?

- Have you ever been surprised by someone telling about a family member or close personal friend with mental illness?

- Do you trust that medical experts always make the right decisions?

- In a family with one disabled child and other normal children, where should the resources (money, time, attention) go – to the child who needs the most help or to the one with the greatest chance of survival or success? (the Sophie's Choice question)

- Barb's mental health improves steadily through the year covered in Part II. What do you think happened after that? Do you think she continued to improve or did she plateau?

- When you started this book did you think it was possible to recover, even partly, from schizophrenia? What about now?

- What do you think about the continued stigma regarding mental illness in our culture? Fifty or sixty years ago, people were reluctant to talk about cancer and kept a cancer diagnosis a secret. Clearly that has changed. Do you think it's possible that the same cultural change would happen about schizophrenia? What makes you think it is likely or unlikely? What would have to change?

- What questions were you left with about Barb's condition?

ABOUT THE AUTHOR

Margaret Hawkins is a writer, critic, curator and educator whose reviews and essays have appeared in the *Chicago Sun-Times*, *ARTnews* and other publications for over twenty years. She currently teaches writing in the Art History and the New Arts Journalism departments at the School of the Art Institute of Chicago.

Hawkins is the author of two novels, *A Year of Cats and Dogs* and *How to Survive a Natural Disaster*.

TO OUR READERS

Conari Press, an imprint of Red Wheel/Weiser, publishes books on topics ranging from spirituality, personal growth, and relationships to women's issues, parenting, and social issues. Our mission is to publish quality books that will make a difference in people's lives-- how we feel about ourselves and how we relate to one another. We value integrity, compassion, and receptivity, both in the books we publish and in the way we do business.

Our readers are our most important resources, and we value your input, suggestions, and ideas about what you would like to see published. Please feel free to contact us, to request our latest book catalog, or to be added to our mailing list.

Conari Press
An imprint of Red Wheel/Weiser, LLC
665 Third Street, Suite 400
San Francisco, CA 94107
www.redwheelweiser.com